Politics of Affect

Politics of All...?

Politics of Affect

Brian Massumi

polity

First published in 2015 by Polity Press

Polity Press
65 Bridge Street
Cambridge CB2 1UR, UK

Polity Press
350 Main Street
Malden, MA 02148, USA

ISBN-13: 978-0-7456-8981-4
ISBN-13: 978-0-7456-8982-1(pb)

A catalogue record for this book is available from the British Library.

Library of Congress Cataloging-in-Publication Data

Massumi, Brian.
   The politics of affect / Brian Massumi.
      pages cm
   Includes bibliographical references and index.
   ISBN 978-0-7456-8981-4 (hardcover : alk. paper) – ISBN 0-7456-8981-7
(hardcover : alk. paper) – ISBN 978-0-7456-8982-1 (pbk. : alk. paper) – ISBN
0-7456-8982-5 (pbk. : alk. paper)   1. Affect (Psychology)   2. Political psychology.
I. Title.
   BF531.M324 2015
   128′.3–dc23

                                                               2014043773

Typeset in 11 on 14 pt Sabon
by Toppan Best-set Premedia Limited
Printed and Bound in the UK by CPI Group (UK) Ltd, Croydon,
CR0 4YY

For further information on Polity, visit our website: politybooks.com

Contents

v

Contents

thinking through affect

*(for thinking through intensity of feeling
that falls life, form life ...)*

Preface

→ *reflecting*
→ *thought taking the plunge*

⟶ *affect as enacted*

The 'politics of affect': the phrase is somewhat redun-
dant. Affect, as it is conceived in this book, is not a
discipline of study of which the politics of affect would
be a subdiscipline. It is a dimension of life – including
of writing, including of reading – which directly carries
a political valence.

The interviews that follow do not purport to present
a comprehensive treatment of the field of affect. Neither
do they present an introductory encapsulation – although
it is hoped that the dialogic format renders the ins and
out of affect more immediately accessible than the academic format. They are an invitation to voyage. Their
aim is to map a passage for thinking through the intensities of feeling that fill life, and form it, across its ups
and downs. Thinking *through* affect is not just reflecting
on it. It is thought taking the plunge, consenting to
ride the waves of affect on a crest of words, drenched
to the conceptual bone in the fineness of its spray. Affect
is only understood as enacted. This book hopes to

enact affect conceptually for the reader through its stream of words.

The account developed here makes no claim to objectivity or general applicability. What would an objective or general approach bring to the singular qualities of life that compose its affective dimension? Stilling. Dullening. Dead disciplinary reckoning. The aim is not to convince with claims of validity, but rather to convey something of the vivacity of the topic: to invite and to incite the reader towards thought experiences pitching off-chart from the pages of the book, on a course of their own beyond its ken. To 'think through' affect is to continue its life-filling, life-forming journey. A concept, Gilles Deleuze once said, is lived or it is nothing.

The angle of approach pursued here can be described as that of process philosophy in its widest sense. What the thinkers to whose work the discussions regularly return – Henri Bergson, William James, Alfred North Whitehead, Gilbert Simondon, Félix Guattari, Gilles Deleuze – have in common is construing the task of philosophy as understanding the world as an ongoing process in continual transformation. It is not concerned with things – certainly not 'in themselves' – so much as with things-in-the-making, in James's famous phrase. It takes change as primary, and sees the regularities of life as temporary barrier islands of stability in stormy seas. This is the first sense in which the process philosophy take on affect carries a political dimension: what it is primarily about is change. The concept of affect is politically oriented from the get go. But moving it onto a 'properly' political register – the arena of social order and reorderings, of settlement and resistance, of clampdowns and uprisings – is not automatic. Affect is proto-political. It concerns the first stirrings of the political, flush with the felt intensities of life. Its politics must be brought out. The conceptual project running through this book is to bring out the politicality of affect, constructing for it an expression that honours its processuality.

The immediately political dimension is also built into the base definition of affect informing process approaches like the one enacted through these interviews. This definition, deceptively simple, was formulated by Spinoza: affect is the power 'to affect and be affected'. This definition recurs throughout the book like a refrain. Each time it occurs, it calls forth helper concepts, in increasing variety. These also recur, and together they begin to weave a conceptual web for thinking through affect. The formula 'to affect and be affected' is also proto-political in the sense that it includes relation in the definition. To affect and to be affected is to be open to the world, to be active in it and to be patient for its return activity. This openness is also taken as primary. It is the cutting edge of change. It is through it that things-in-the-making cut their transformational teeth. One always affects and is affected in encounters; which is to say, through events. To begin affectively in change is to begin in relation, and to begin in relation is to begin in the event.

This brief itinerary already illustrates a characteristic of the processual concept of affect that distinguishes it from the general ideas that are the standard currency of thought, and upon which the traditional disciplines of knowledge are built. The concept of affect is 'transversal', in Deleuze and Guattari's understanding of that term. This means that it cuts across the usual categories. Prime among these are the categories of the subjective and the objective. Although affect is all about intensities of feeling, the feeling process cannot be characterized as exclusively subjective or objective: the encounters through which it passes strike the body as immediately as they stir the mind. It involves subjective qualities as directly as the objects provoking them, or with which they move. It concerns desire as much as what is imperatively given; freedom as much as constraint. Thinking the transversality of affect requires that we fundamentally rethink all of these categories in ways that include them in the event, together. It requires honing concepts for the mutual inclusion in the event of elements usually separated out from it, and from each other. A simple mix and match of received categories is not enough. An integral reforging is necessary. This is complicated by the fact that although affect's openness is unconfinable in the interiority of a subject, to take one of the concepts in need of restaging, it is at the same time formative of subjects. Although affect fundamentally concerns relations in encounter, it is at the same time positively productive of the individualities in relation. In its transversality, affect is strangely polyvalent.

Much of the work of the book is dedicated to laying the polyvalent groundwork for this reforging of concepts, transversal to their usual diametric opposition with each other. Such fellow-travelling concepts as 'differential affective attunement', 'collective individuation', 'micropolitics', 'thinking-feeling', 'bare activity', 'ontopower' and 'immanent critique' relay the base

Use This in DISS.

definition of affect with which the first interview begins. Once they introduce themselves, they wend their way through subsequent interviews, taking on greater conceptual consistency, complexifying the concept of affect as they go. This is what a process-oriented exploration does: complexify its conceptual web as it advances. It tries not to reduce. It tries not to encapsulate. It does not end in an overview. Rather, it works to become more and more adequate to the ongoing complexity of life. This means that it does not arrive at any final answers. It does not even seek solutions. It seeks to re-pose the problems life poses itself, always under transformation. The goal is to arrive at a transformational matrix of concepts apt to continue the open-ended voyage of thinking-feeling life's processual qualities, foregrounding their proto-political dimension and the paths by which it comes to full expression in politics (taking the word in the plural).

The interviews included in this book are not just dialogues. They are themselves encounters. The interlocutors are not just questioners, they are accomplices in thought. The interviews typically took place against the background of preparatory exchanges that primed the thinking they would bring to expression. In some cases (chapters 4 and 5), they arose in the context of active collaborations in processual thinking and its political prolongations. These event-based explorations were carried out in the context of the SenseLab, a 'laboratory for research-creation' based in Montreal that operates transversally between philosophy, creative practice and activism. My years of involvement in the SenseLab have inestimably enriched my thinking, and my life. The encounters and relations I have experienced in connection with the SenseLab have been transformative – none more so than those with SenseLab founder Erin Manning, my prime accomplice in thinking (and everything else). This book is dedicated to her.

Yubraj Aryal is a Visiting Lecturer in the Comparative Literature and Philosophy and Literature Program at Purdue University, USA. He is also the editor of *Journal of Philosophy: A Cross-Disciplinary Inquiry*. He has conducted interviews for the journal of leading thinkers such as Richard Rorty, Hilary Putnam, Kwame Anthony Appiah, Marjorie Perloff, Charles Altieri, Robert Young and Laurent Berlant, among others.

Arno Boehler is Associate Professor in the Department of Philosophy at the University of Vienna, Austria. He is the founder of the philosophy performance festival 'Philosophy On Stage'. He leads the research project 'Artist-Philosophers: Philosophy AS Arts-Based-Research', University of Applied Arts Vienna, sponsored by the Austrian Science Fund. He has held fellowships at the Universities of Bangalore, Heidelberg, New York, and Princeton. Further information: http://homepage.univie.ac.at/arno.boehler

Christoph Brunner is a researcher at the Institute for Contemporary Art Research, Zurich University of the Arts, Switzerland. His work addresses the relay between cultural and media theory and current discourses on research-creation. His PhD dissertation, 'Ecologies of Relation: Collectivity in Art and Media', investigates new forms of collectivity in aesthetic practices between art, media and activism. In 2012 he co-edited the book

Practices of Experimentation: Research and Teaching in the Arts Today. He is a participant in the SenseLab and a researcher on the SenseLab's 'Immediations: Media, Art, Event' international partnership project, and serves on the editorial board of *Inflexions: A Journal for Research-Creation*.

Jonas Fritsch is Assistant Professor in the Department of Aesthetics and Communication, Aarhus University, Denmark. His research centres on a creative thinking of interaction design and affect theory through practical design experiments carried out at the Centre for Advanced Visualization and Interaction (CAVI) and the Centre for Participatory IT (PIT) at Aarhus. He is a participant in the SenseLab and a researcher on the SenseLab's 'Immediations: Media, Art, Event' international partnership project, and serves on the editorial boards of *Inflexions: A Journal for Research-Creation* and *Conjunctions: Transdisciplinary Journal of Cultural Participation*.

Erin Manning holds a University Research Chair in Relational Art and Philosophy in the Faculty of Fine Arts at Concordia University, Montreal, Canada. She is also the director of the SenseLab (www.senselab.ca), a laboratory that explores the intersections between art practice and philosophy through the matrix of the sensing body in movement. Her current art practice is centred on large-scale participatory installations that facilitate emergent collectivities. Current art projects are focused on the concept of 'minor gestures' in relation to colour, movement and participation. Publications include *Always More Than One: Individuation's Dance*

(2013), *Relationscapes: Movement, Art, Philosophy* (2009) and, with Brian Massumi, *Thought in the Act: Passages in the Ecology of Experience* (2014). Forthcoming book projects include a translation of Fernand Deligny's *Les détours de l'agir ou le moindre geste* and a monograph entitled *The Minor Gesture*. She is the founder of the SenseLab and founding editor of *Inflexions: A Journal for Research-Creation*.

Joel McKim is Lecturer in Media and Cultural Studies in the Department of Film, Media and Cultural Studies at Birkbeck, University of London, UK. His research is concerned with issues of political communication in the built environment and the intersection of media and architecture. His recent writing on these topics has appeared in such journals as *Theory, Culture & Society*, *Space and Culture*, *PUBLIC* and *borderlands* and in the edited collections *DIY Citizenship: Critical Making and Social Media* (2014) and *The Missed Encounter of Radical Philosophy with Architecture* (2014). He is currently completing a book entitled *Memory Complex: Architecture, Media and Politics in a Post-9/11 New York*.

Bodil Marie Stavning Thomsen is Associate Professor in the Department of Aesthetics and Communication, Aarhus University, Denmark. Her research is in the fields of art, culture and media (film, fashion, art video, interfaces and film, especially the haptic compositions of Lars von Trier's works). Her publications in English have appeared in a number of edited volumes including *Performing Archives/Archives of Performance* (2013), *A Cultural History of the Avant-Garde in the Nordic*

Preface

Countries (2013) and *Globalizing Art* (2011). She is a participant in the SenseLab and a researcher on the SenseLab's 'Immediations: Media, Art, Event' international partnership project. She serves on the editorial board of *Inflexions: A Journal for Research-Creation* and is currently Deputy Editor-in-Chief of the *Journal of Aesthetics and Culture*.

Mary Zournazi is an Australian author, philosopher, film maker and playwright. She teaches at the University of New South Wales, Australia. She is the author of several books including *Hope: New Philosophies for Change* (2003), *Keywords to War* (2007) and, most recently, *Inventing Peace* (2013), which is co-authored with internationally acclaimed German film director Wim Wenders.

The interviews in this book have previously appeared in the following publications:

Chapter 1: *Hope: New Philosophies for Change.* Ed. Mary Zournazi. New York: Routledge; London: Lawrence & Wishart; Sydney: Pluto Press Australia, 2002–3, pp. 210–42.
Chapter 2: *Inflexions: A Journal for Research Creation* (Montréal), no. 3 (October 2009), www.inflexions.org
Chapter 3: *Journal of Philosophy: A Cross-Disciplinary Inquiry* (Katmandu), vol. 7, no. 18 (fall 2013), pp. 64–76, under the original title "Affect, capitalism, and resistance".
Chapter 4: *Peripeti: Tidsskrift for dramaturgiske studier* (Copenhagen), no. 27 (2012), pp. 89–96 (abridged version).

Chapter 5: *Ästhetik der Existenz: Lebensformen im Widerstreit*. Ed. Elke Bippus, Jörg Huber and Roberto Negro. Zurich: Institut für Theorie/Edition Vodemeer, 2013, pp. 135–50, under the original title "Fields of Potential: Affective Immediacy, Anxiety, and the Necessities of Life".

Chapter 6: *Wissen wir, was ein Körper vermag?* Ed. Arno Boehler, Krassimira Kruschkova and Susanne Valerie Granzer. Bielefeld: Transcript Verlag, 2014, pp. 23–42.

I
Navigating movements

Mary Zournazi*: I'd like to think about hope and the affective dimensions of experience – what freedoms are possible in the new and 'virtualized' global and political economies that frame our lives. To begin, though, what are your thoughts on the potential of hope for these times?

Brian Massumi: From my own point of view, the way that a concept like hope can be made useful is when it is not connected to an expected success – when it starts to be something different from optimism – because when you start trying to think ahead into the future from the present point, rationally there really isn't much room for hope. Globally it's a very pessimistic affair, with economic inequalities increasing year by year, with health and sanitation levels steadily decreasing in

* Interview by Mary Zournazi (2001)

---

many regions, with the global effects of environmental deterioration already being felt, with conflicts among nations and peoples apparently only getting more intractable, leading to mass displacements of workers and refugees...It seems such a mess that it can be paralysing. If hope is the opposite of pessimism, then there's precious little to be had. On the other hand, if hope is separated from concepts of optimism and pessimism, from a wishful projection of success or even some kind of a rational calculation of outcomes, then I think it starts to be interesting – because it places it in the present.

Mary Zournazi: Yes – the idea of hope in the present is vital. Otherwise we endlessly look to the future or towards some utopian dream of a better society or life, which can only leave us disappointed, and if we see pessimism as the natural flow from this, we can only be paralysed as you suggest.

Brian Massumi: That's right, because in every situation there are any number of levels of organization and tendencies in play, in co-operation with each other or at cross-purposes. The way all the elements interrelate is so complex that it isn't necessarily comprehensible in one go. There's always a sort of vagueness surrounding the situation, an uncertainty about where you might be able to go and what you might be able to do once you exit that particular context. This uncertainty can actually be empowering – once you realize that it gives you a margin of manoeuvrability and you focus on that, rather than on projecting success or failure. It gives you the feeling that there is always an opening to experiment, to try and see. This brings a sense of potential to the situation. The present's 'boundary condition', to borrow a phrase from science, is never a closed door. It is an open threshold – a threshold of potential. You are only ever in the present in passing. If you look at it that way you don't have to feel boxed in, no matter what horrors are afield and no matter what, rationally, you expect will come. You may not reach the end of the trail but at least there's a next step. The question of which next step to take is a lot less intimidating than how to reach a far-off goal in a distant future where all our problems will finally be solved. It's utopian thinking, for me, that's 'hopeless'.

Mary Zournazi: So how do your ideas on 'affect' and hope come together here?

Brian Massumi: In my own work I use the concept of 'affect' as a way of talking about that margin of manoeuvrability, the 'where we might be able to go and what we might be able to do' in every present situation. I guess 'affect' is the word I use for 'hope'. One of the reasons it's such an important concept for me is because it explains why focusing on the next experimental step rather than the big utopian picture isn't really settling for less. It's not exactly going for more, either. It's more like being right where you are – more intensely. To get from affect to intensity you have to understand affect as something other than simply a personal feeling. By 'affect' I don't mean 'emotion' in the everyday sense. The way I use it comes primarily from Spinoza. He talks of the body in terms of its capacity for affecting or being affected. These are not two different capacities – they always go together. When you affect something, you are at the same time opening yourself up to being affected in turn, and in a slightly different way than you might have been the moment before. You have made a transition, however slight. You have stepped over a threshold. Affect is this passing of a threshold, seen from the point of view of the change in capacity. It's crucial to remember that Spinoza uses this to talk about the body. What a body is, he says, is what it can do as it goes along. This is a totally pragmatic definition. A body is defined by what capacities it carries from step to step. What these are exactly is changing constantly. A body's ability to affect or be affected – its charge of affect – isn't something fixed.

So depending on the circumstances, it goes up and down gently like a tide, or maybe storms and crests like a wave, or at times simply bottoms out. It's because this is all attached to the movements of the body that it can't be reduced to emotion. It's not just subjective, which is not to say that there is nothing subjective about it. Spinoza says that every transition is accompanied by a feeling of the change in capacity. The affect and the feeling of the transition are not two different things. They're two sides of the same coin, just like affecting and being affected. That's the first sense in which affect is about intensity – every affect is a doubling. The experience of a change, an affecting-being affected, is redoubled by an experience of the experience. This gives the body's movements a kind of depth that stays with it across all its transitions – accumulating in memory, in habit, in reflex, in desire, in tendency. Emotion is the way the depth of that ongoing experience registers personally at a given moment.

4

Mary Zournazi: Emotion, then, is only a limited expression of the 'depth' of our experience?

Brian Massumi: Well, an emotion is a very partial expression of affect. It only draws on a limited selection of memories and only activates certain reflexes or tendencies, for example. No one emotional state can encompass all the depth and breadth of our experiencing of experiencing – all the ways our experience redoubles itself. The same thing could be said for conscious thought. So when we feel a particular emotion or think a particular thought, where have all the other memories, habits, tendencies gone that might have come at the point? And where have the bodily capacities for affecting and being affected that they're inseparable from gone? There's no way they can all be actually expressed at any given point. But they're not totally absent either, because a different selection of them is sure to come up at the next step. They're still there, but virtually – in potential. Affect as a whole, then, is the virtual co-presence of potentials.

This is the second way that affect has to do with intensity. There's like a population or swarm of potential ways of affecting or being affected that follows along as we move through life. We always have a vague sense that they're there. That vague sense of potential, we call it our 'freedom', and defend it fiercely. But no matter how certainly we know that the potential is there, it always seems just out of reach, or maybe around the next bend. Because it isn't actually there – only virtually. But maybe if we can take little, practical, experimental, strategic measures to expand our emotional register, or limber up our thinking, we can access more of our potential at each step, have more of it actually available. Having more potentials available intensifies our life. We're not enslaved by our situations. Even if we never have our freedom, we're always experiencing a degree of freedom, or 'wriggle room'. Our degree of freedom at any one time corresponds to how much of our experiential 'depth' we can access towards a next step – how intensely we are living and moving.

Once again it's all about the openness of situations and how we can live that openness. And you have to remember that the way we live it is always entirely embodied, and that is never entirely personal – it's never all contained in our emotions and conscious thoughts. That's a way of saying it's not just about us, in isolation. In affect, we are never alone. That's because affects in Spinoza's definition are basically ways of connecting, to others and to other situations. They are our angle of participation in processes larger than ourselves. With intensified affect comes a stronger sense of embeddedness in a larger field of life – a heightened sense of belonging, with other people and to other places. Spinoza takes us quite far, but for me his thought needs to be supplemented with the work of thinkers like Henri Bergson, who focuses on the intensities of experience, and William James, who focuses on their connectedness.

Mary Zournazi: When you were just talking about Spinoza and the way you understand affect, I don't want to put a false determination on it, but is it a more primal sense of the capacity to be human and how we feel connections to the world and others? That's almost natural to a certain extent...

Brian Massumi: I wouldn't tend to say it's primal, if that means more 'natural'. I don't think affective intensity is any more natural than the ability to stand back and reflect on something, or the ability to pin something down in language. But I guess that it might be considered primal in the sense that it is direct. You don't need a concept of 'mediation' to talk about it. In cultural theory, people often talk as if the body and its situatedness on the one hand, and our emotions, thoughts and the language we use for them on the other, are totally different realities, as if there has to be something to come between them and put them into touch with each other. Theories of ideology are designed for this. Mediation, in whatever guise it appears, is the way a lot of theorists try to overcome the old Cartesian duality between mind and body, but it actually leaves it in place and just tries to build a bridge between them. But if you define affect the way we just did, then obviously it includes very elaborated functions like language. There's an affect associated with every functioning of the body, from moving your foot to take a step to moving your lips to make words. Affect is simply a body movement looked at from the point of view of its potential – its capacity to come to be, or better, to come to do. It has to do with modes of activity, and what manner of capacities they carry forward.

Like I said, the directness I'm talking about isn't necessarily a self-presence or self-possession, which is how we normally tend to think of our freedom. If it's direct, it's in the sense that it's directly in transition – in the body passing out of the present moment and the situation it's in, towards the next one. But it's also the doubling of the body in the situation – its doubling over into what it might have been or done if it had contrived to live that transition more intensely. A body doesn't coincide with itself. It's not present to itself. It is already on the move to a next, at the same time as it is doubling over on itself, bringing its past up to date in the present, through memory, habit, reflex and so on. Which means you can't even say that a body ever coincides with its affective dimension. It is selecting from it, extracting and actualizing certain potentials from it. You can think of affect in the broadest sense as what remains of the potential after each or every thing a body says or does – as a perpetual bodily remainder. Looked at from a different angle, this perpetual remainder is an excess. It's like a reserve of potential or newness or creativity that is experienced alongside every actual production of meaning in language or in any performance of a useful function – vaguely but directly experienced, as something more, a more to come, a life overspilling as it gathers itself up to move on.

Mary Zournazi: What immediately comes to mind is something like anger. It's a very strong bodily experience, a heat-of-the-moment intensity – it doesn't seem to have a positive charge in some ways, you know, because it is often a reaction against something...

Brian Massumi: I think affective expressions like anger and laughter are perhaps the most powerful because they interrupt a situation. They are negative in that sense. They interrupt the flow of meaning that's taking place: the normalized interrelations and interactions that are happening and the functions that are being fulfilled. Because of that, they are irruptions of something that doesn't fit. Anger, for example, forces the situation to attention, it forces a pause filled with an intensity that is often too extreme to be expressed in words. Anger often degenerates into noise and inarticulate gestures. This forces the situation to rearray itself around that irruption, and to deal with the intensity in one way or another. In that sense it's brought something positive out – a reconfiguration.

There's always an instantaneous calculation or judgement that takes place as to how you respond to an outburst of anger. But it's not a judgement in the sense that you've gone through all the possibilities and thought it through explicitly – you don't have time for that kind of thing. Instead you use a kind of judgement that takes place instantly and brings your entire body into the situation. The response to anger is usually as gestural as the outburst of anger itself. The overload of the situation is such that, even if you refrain from a gesture, that itself is a gesture. An outburst of anger brings a number of outcomes into direct presence to one another – there could be a peace-making or a move towards violence, there could be a breaking of relations, all the possibilities are present, packed into the present moment. It all happens, again, before there is time for much reflection, if any. So there's a kind of thought that is taking place in the body, through a kind of instantaneous assessment of affect, an assessment of potential directions and situational outcomes that isn't separate from our immediate, physical acting-out of our implication in the situation. The philosopher C.S. Peirce had a word for thought that is still couched in bodily feeling, that is still fully bound up with unfolding sensation as it goes into action but before it has been able to articulate itself in conscious reflection and guarded language. He called it 'abduction'.

Mary Zournazi: Right, right. Oh, that's like a kind of capture...

Brian Massumi: Yes, I think you could say that sensation is the registering of affect that I referred to before – the passing awareness of being at a threshold – and that affect is thinking, bodily – consciously but vaguely, in the sense that is not yet a fully formed thought. It's a movement of thought, or a thinking movement. There are certain logical categories, like abduction, that could be used to describe this.

Mary Zournazi: I think of abduction as a kind of stealing of the moment. It has a wide range of meanings too – it could be stealing or it could be an alien force or possession...

Brian Massumi: Or it could be you drawn in by the situation, captured by it, by its eventfulness, rather than you capturing it. But this capture by the situation is not necessarily an oppression. It could be...

Mary Zournazi: It could be the kind of freedom we were just talking about...

Brian Massumi: Exactly, it could be accompanied by a sense of vitality or vivacity, a sense of being more alive. That's a lot more compelling than coming to 'correct' conclusions or assessing outcomes, although it can also bring results. It might force you to find a margin, a manoeuvre you didn't know you had, and couldn't have just thought your way into. It can change you, expand you. That's what being alive is all about.

So you can't put positive or negative connotations on affect. That would be to judge it from the outside. It would be going in a moralizing direction. Spinoza makes a distinction between a morality and an ethics. To move in an ethical direction, from a Spinozan point of view, is not to attach positive or negative values to actions based on a characterization or classification of them according to a pre-set system of judgement. It means assessing what kind of potential they tap into and express. Whether a person is going to joke or get angry when they are in a tight spot, that uncertainty produces an affective change in the situation. That affective loading and how it plays out is an ethical act, because it affects where people might go or what they might do as a result. It has consequences.

Mary Zournazi: Ethics, then, is always situational?

Brian Massumi: Ethics in this sense is completely situational. It's completely pragmatic. And it happens between people, in the social gaps. There is no intrinsic good or evil. The ethical value of an action is what it brings out in the situation, for its transformation, how it breaks sociality open. Ethics is about how we inhabit uncertainty, together. It's not about judging each other right or wrong. For Nietzsche, like Spinoza, there is still a distinction between good and bad even if there's not one between good and evil. Basically the 'good' is affectively defined as what brings maximum potential and connection to the situation. It is defined in terms of becoming.

Mary Zournazi: This makes me think of your idea of 'walking as controlled falling'. In some ways, every step that we take works with gravity so we don't fall, but it's not something we consciously think about, because our body is already moving and is full of both constraint and freedom. I found it interesting because, in some other ways, I've been trying to think about another relationship – between perception and language – and it seems to me that 'affect' and this notion of body movement can provide a more integrated and vital way of talking about experience and language.

Brian Massumi: I like the notion of 'walking as controlled falling'. It's something of a proverb, and Laurie Anderson, among others, has used it. It conveys the sense that freedom, or the ability to move forward and to transit through life, isn't necessarily about escaping from constraints. There are always constraints. When we walk, we're dealing with the constraint of gravity. There's also the constraint of balance, and a need for equilibrium. But, at the same time, to walk you need to throw off the equilibrium, you have to let yourself almost go into a fall, then you cut it off and regain the balance. You move forward by playing with the constraints, not avoiding them. There's an openness of movement, even though there's no escaping constraint. It's similar with language. I see it as a play between constraint and room to manoeuvre. If you think of language in the traditional way, as a correspondence between a word with its established meaning on the one

hand and a matching perception on the other, then it
starts coagulating. It's just being used as a totally conventional system for pointing out things you want other
people to recognize. It's all about pointing out what
everyone can agree is already there. When you think
about it, though, there's a unique feeling to every experience that comes along, and the exact details of it can
never be exhausted by linguistic expression. That's
partly because no two people in the same situation will
have had exactly the same experience of it – they would
be able to argue and discuss the nuances endlessly. And
it's partly because there was just too much there between
them to be completely articulated – especially if you
think about what was only there potentially, or virtually. But there are uses of language that can bring that
inadequation between language and experience to the
fore in a way that can convey the 'too much' of the situation – its charge – in a way that actually fosters new
experiences.

Humour is a prime example. So is poetic expression,
taken in its broadest sense. So language is two-pronged:
it is a capture of experience, it codifies and normalizes
it and makes it communicable by providing a neutral
frame of reference. But at the same time it can convey
what I would call 'singularities of experience', the
kinds of affective movements we were talking about
before that are totally situation-specific, but in an open
kind of way. Experiencing this potential for change,
experiencing the eventfulness and uniqueness of every
situation, even the most conventional ones, that's not
necessarily about commanding movement, it's about
navigating movement. It's about being immersed in an
experience that is already under way. It's about being

bodily attuned to opportunities in the movement, going with the flow. It's more like surfing the situation, or tweaking it, than commanding or programming it. The command paradigm approaches experience as if we were somehow outside it, looking in, like disembodied subjects handling an object. But our experiences aren't objects. They're us, they're what we're made of. We are our situations, we are our moving through them. We are our participation – not some abstract entity that is somehow outside looking in at it all.

Mary Zournazi: The movement in language is important and it opens another door or window to perception. But I suppose, as intellectuals, there is the problem of the codification of language within critical discourse and theoretical writing – where that language can stop movement and it can express everything in particular terms or methods that cut off the potential of understanding freedom or experience...

Brian Massumi: 'Critical' practices aimed at increasing potentials for freedom and for movement are inadequate, because in order to critique something in any kind of definitive way you have to pin it down. In a way it is an almost sadistic enterprise that separates something out, attributes set characteristics to it, then applies a final judgement to it – objectifies it, in a moralizing kind of way. I understand that using a 'critical method' is not the same as 'being critical'. But still I think there is always that moralizing undertone to critique. Because of that, I think, it loses contact with other more moving dimensions of experience. It doesn't allow for other kinds of practices that might not have so much to do with mastery and judgement as with affective connection and abductive participation.

Mary Zournazi: The non-judgemental is interesting, you know, because you are always somehow implicated in trying to make judgements...To not make judgements in critical thought is a very hard thing to do. It takes a lot of courage to move in that direction, because otherwise...

Brian Massumi: Well, it requires a willingness to take risks, to make mistakes and even to come across as silly. Critique is not amenable to that. And it suffers as a consequence. A critical perspective that tries to come to a definitive judgement on something is always in some way a failure, because it is happening at a remove from the process it's judging. Something could have happened in the intervening time, or something barely perceptible might have been happening away from the centre of critical focus. These developments may become important later. The process of pinning down and separating out is also a weakness in judgement, because it doesn't allow for these seeds of change, connections in the making that might not be activated or obvious at the moment. Being attuned to these possibilities requires being willing to take risks. In a sense, judgemental reason is an extremely weak form of thought, precisely because it is so sure of itself. This is not to say that it shouldn't be used. But I think it should be complemented by other practices of thought, it shouldn't be relied on exclusively. It's limiting if it's the only or even the primary stance of the intellectual.

———

A case in point is the anti-globalization movement. It's easy to find weaknesses in it, in its tactics or in its analysis of capitalism. But if you wait around for a movement to come along that corresponds to your particular image of the correct approach, you'll be waiting your life away. Nothing is ever that neat. But luckily people didn't wait around. They jumped right in and started experimenting and networking, step by step. As a result, new connections have been made between people and movements operating in different regions of the world, on different political levels, from the most local grassroots levels up to the most established NGOs, using different organizational structures. In a very short period of time the entire discourse surrounding globalization has shifted. Actually, not only surrounding it but inside its institutions also – it's now impossible for an international meeting to take place without issues of poverty and health being on the agenda. It's far from a solution, but it's a start. It's ongoing. That's the point: to keep on going.

Mary Zournazi: The idea of 'controlled walking' is a good example of what you were just talking about in terms of the limitations on the self and the freedoms that are possible. But I am also thinking about it as relating to the idea of 'societies of control' – which you have written about. We now live in societies of control, so how do control and power in this new age also offer the possibility of freedom?

Brian Massumi: In physics there is a very famous problem that heavily influenced the development of chaos theory. It's called the 'three-body problem', where you have completely deterministic trajectories of bodies constrained by Newtonian laws. For example, if you have two bodies interacting, through gravity for example, everything is calculable and foreseeable.

If you know where they are in relation to each at one moment, you can project a path and figure out where they were at any given moment in the past, or at a time in the future. But if you have three of them together what happens is that a margin of unpredictability creeps in. The paths can't be accurately determined after a point. They can turn erratic, ending up at totally different places than you'd expect. What has happened? How can chance creep into a totally deterministic system? It's not that the bodies have somehow broken the laws of physics. What happens is interference, or resonation. It's not really discrete bodies and paths interacting. It's fields. Gravity is a field – a field of potential attraction, collision, orbit, of potential centripetal and centrifugal movements. All these potentials form such complex interference patterns when three fields overlap that a measure of indeterminacy creeps in. It's not that we just don't have a detailed enough knowledge to predict. Accurate prediction is impossible because the indeterminacy is objective. So there's an objective degree of freedom even in the most deterministic system. Something in the coming-together of movements, even according to the strictest of laws, flips the constraints over into conditions of freedom. It's a relational effect, a complexity effect. Affect is like our human gravitational field, and what we call our freedom is its relational flips. Freedom is not about breaking or escaping constraints. It's about flipping them over into degrees of freedom. You can't really escape the constraints. No body can escape gravity. Laws are part of what we are, they're intrinsic to our identities. No human can simply escape gender, for example. The cultural 'laws' of gender are part of what makes us who we are, they're part of the process that produced us as individuals. You can't just step out of gender identity. But just maybe you can take steps to encourage gender to flip. That can't be an individual undertaking. It involves tweaking the interference and resonation patterns between individuals. It's a relational undertaking. You're not acting on yourself or other individuals separately. You're acting on them together, on their togetherness, their field of belonging. The idea is that there are ways of acting upon the level of belonging itself, on the moving together and coming together of bodies per se. This would have to involve an evaluation of collective potential that would be ethical in the sense we were talking about before. It would be a caring for the relating of things as such – a politics of belonging instead of a politics of identity, of correlated emergence instead of separate domains of interest attracting each other or colliding in predictable ways. In Isabelle Stengers's terms this kind of politics is an ecology of practices. It's a pragmatic politics of the in-between. For me, it's an abductive politics that has to operate on the level of affect.

Mary Zournazi: So what does this political ecology involve?

Brian Massumi: To move towards that kind of political ecology you have to get rid of the idea as power or constraint as power over. It's always a power to. The greatest power of the law is the power to form us. Power doesn't just force us down certain paths, it puts the paths in us, so by the time we learn to follow its constraints we're following ourselves. The effects of power on us are our identity. That's what Michel Foucault taught us. If power just came at us from outside, if it was just an extrinsic relation, it would be simple. You'd just run away. In the 1960s and 1970s that's how a lot of people looked at it – including myself. Drop out, stop following the predictable, straight-and-narrow path, and things like sexism will just disappear. Well, they didn't. It's a lot more complicated than that. Power comes up into us from the field of potential. It 'in-forms' us, it's intrinsic to our formation, it's part of our emergence as identified individuals, and it emerges with us – we actualize it, as it in-forms us. So in a way it's as potentializing as what we call freedom, only what it potentializes is limited to a number of predictable paths. It's the calculable part of affect, the most probable next steps and eventual outcomes. As Foucault says, power is productive, and it produces not so much repressions as regularities. Which brings us to the 'society of control' and to capitalism...

Mary Zournazi: I was just going to ask you about that...

Brian Massumi: It is very clear that capitalism has undergone a major reconfiguration since the Second World War, and it's been very difficult to think through what that has been. For me the most useful way of thinking about it comes from the post-Autonomia Italian Marxist movement, in particular the thought of Antonio Negri. The argument is that capitalist powers have pretty much abandoned control in the sense of 'power over'. That corresponds to the first flush of 'disciplinary' power in Michel Foucault's vocabulary. Disciplinary power starts by enclosing bodies in top-down institutions – prisons, asylums, hospitals, schools and so on. It encloses in order to find ways of producing more regularity in behaviour. Its aim is to manufacture normality – good, healthy citizens. As top-down disciplinary power takes hold and spreads, it finds ways of doing the same thing without the enclosure. Prisons spawn halfway houses, hospitals spawn community clinics and home-care, educational institutions spawn the self-help and career retooling industries. It starts operating in an open field. After a certain point it starts paying more attention to the relays between the points in that field, the transitions between institutions, than to the institutions themselves. It's seeped into the in-between. At this point it starts to act directly on the kinds of interference and resonation effects I was just mentioning. It starts working directly on bodies' movements and momentum, producing momentums, the more varied and even erratic the better. Normality starts to lose its hold. The regularities start to loosen. This loosening of normality is part of capitalism's dynamic. It's not a simple liberation. It's capitalism's own form of power. It's no longer disciplinary institutional power that defines everything, it's capitalism's power to produce variety – because markets get saturated. Produce variety and you produce a niche market. The oddest of affective tendencies are OK – as long as they pay. Capitalism starts intensifying or diversifying affect, but only in order to extract surplus-value. It hijacks affect in order to intensify profit potential. It literally valorizes affect. The capitalist logic of surplus-value production starts to take over the relational field that is also the domain of political ecology, the ethical field of resistance to identity and predictable paths. It's very troubling and confusing, because it seems to me that there's been a certain kind of convergence between the dynamic of capitalist power and the dynamic of resistance.

Mary Zournazi: For me, this raises a question about the way capitalism does capture potential and organizes itself. There are two issues I want to address: firstly, in relationship to the question of hope – human aspirations and hopes are directly related to capitalism today. The natural or 'potential of hope' is seized upon and is tied very much to a monetary system, economic imperatives or questions of ownership. Secondly, the relationship between hope and fear in capitalism. I think that hope and fear are part of the same equation...

Brian Massumi: I think they definitely are. It would help to try to talk a little bit more about the change in capitalism and what that constitutes, and then go back to that question. Thinkers like Negri say that the products of capitalism have become more intangible, they've become more information- and service-based. Material objects and physical commodities that were once the engine of the economy are becoming more and more peripheral, in profit terms. For example, the cost of computers keeps plummeting. It's difficult to make a profit from their manufacture because there's a mass of basically identical versions from different companies, and they're all pretty interchangeable.

Mary Zournazi: Is that mass production in a sense or a different notion of mass production?

Brian Massumi: It is a mass production but it leads to a different kind of production, because what can someone sell if they can't make a profit from the object? What they can sell are services around the object and they can sell the right to do the things you can do through the object. That's why copyright is such a huge issue. The capitalist product is more and more an intellectual property that you buy a right to use, not an object you buy outright. If you buy a software package, often you're not supposed to even make copies of it for yourself, like one for your desktop and one for a laptop. If you buy a book, you own an object. You can resell it, or lend it, or rebind it, or photocopy it for your own use. If you buy a software package, you're not so much buying an object, you're buying a bundle of functions. You're buying the right to use those functions, with all sorts of strings attached. You're basically buying the right to be able to do things, ways of affecting and being affected – word-processing capacities, image-capture and -processing capacities, printing capacities, calculation capacities... It's at the same time very potentializing, and controlled. The 'cutting edge' products are more and more multivalent. 'Convergence' is the buzzword. When you buy a computerized product, you can do a lot of different things with it – you use it to extend your affective capacities. It becomes a motor force of your life – like a turbo charge to your vitality. It enables you to go farther and to do more, to fit more in. The way even older-style products are sold has something to do with this. You don't just buy a car, the dealers tell us, you buy a lifestyle. When you consume, you're not just getting something to use for a particular use, you're getting yourself a life. All products become more intangible, sort of atmospheric, and marketing gets hinged more and more on style and branding...

Mary Zournazi: More meaningless?

Brian Massumi: Possibly, possibly but not necessarily, because, if you think of style or branding, it is an attempt to express what we were talking about before as the sense of vitality or liveliness. It is a selling of experience or lifestyles, and people put themselves together by what they buy and what they can do through what they can buy. So ownership of things is becoming comparatively less important. The centrality of 'conspicuous consumption' belongs to an earlier phase. It's this enabling of experience that is taking over. Now, that enablement of experience has to be tended. Companies work very hard to produce brand loyalty. 'Fidelity programmes' involving things like rewards points are everywhere. The product becomes a long-term part of your life, you're brought into a relationship with the company through fidelity programmes, service networks, promises of upgrades, etc. The way you use the product is also more and more oriented towards relationship – the most seductive products produce possibilities of connection. 'Connectability' is another buzzword. When we buy a product, we're buying potential connections with other things and especially other people – for example, when a family buys a computer to keep in touch by email, or when you get a computer for work and end up joining online communities. What's being sold more and more is experience, social experience. The corporation, the capitalist company, is having to create social networks and cultural nodes that come together around the product, and the product gets used more and more to create social networks that radiate out from it. 'Networking' was the buzzword in the 1980s, when this new kind of capitalist power was just coming into its own. Marketing itself is starting to operate along those lines. There is a new kind of marketing called viral marketing where specialized companies will surf the web to find communities of interest that have spontaneously formed. It started in the music industry, around fan networks for bands. They find a group of people who have a very strong affective attachment to a band or a performer that is very central to how they see themselves and to what they perceive as the quality of their life. They will network with them, offer them tickets or inside information, or special access, and in return the members of the group will agree to take on certain marketing tasks. So the difference between marketing and consuming and between living and buying is becoming smaller and smaller, to the point that they are getting almost indistinguishable. On both the production side and the consumption side it is all about intangible, basically cultural products or products of experience that invariably have a collective dimension to them.

Mary Zournazi: So as consumers we are part of the new networks of global and collective exchange...

Brian Massumi: Individual consumers are being inducted into these collective processes rather than being

separated out and addressed as free agents who are supposed to make an informed consumer choice as rational
individuals. This is a step beyond niche marketing, it's
relational marketing. It works by contagion rather than
by convincing, on affect rather than rational choice. It
works at least as much on the level of our 'indeterminate
sociality' as on the level of our identities. More and
more, what it does is hitch a ride on movements afoot
in the social field, on social stirrings, which it channels
in profit-making directions. People like Negri talk about
the 'social factory', a kind of socialization of capitalism,
where capitalism is more about scouting and capturing
or producing and multiplying potentials for doing
and being than it is about selling *things*. The kind of
work that goes into this he calls 'immaterial labour'.
The product, ultimately, is us. We are in-formed by
capitalist powers of production. Our whole life becomes
a 'capitalist tool' – our vitality, our affective capacities.
It's to the point that our life potentials are indistinguishable from capitalist forces of production. In some of my
essays I've called this the 'subsumption of life' under
capitalism.

Jeremy Rifkin is a social critic who now teaches at
one of the most prestigious business schools in the US
(talk about the capture of resistance!). Rifkin has a
description of capitalism that is actually surprisingly
similar to Negri's. And he's teaching it to the next generation of capitalists. It centres on what he calls 'gatekeeping' functions. Here the figure of power is no longer
the billy club of the policeman, it's the barcode or the
PIN number. These are control mechanisms, but not in
the old sense of 'power over'. It's control in Gilles
Deleuze's sense, which is closer to 'check mechanism'.

It's all about checkpoints. At the grocery store counter, the barcode on what you're buying checks the object out of the store. At the automatic bank teller, the PIN number on your card checks you into your account. The checks don't control you, they don't tell you where to go or what to be doing at any particular time. They don't lord it over you. They just lurk. They lie in wait for you at key points. You come to them, and they're activated by your arrival. You're free to move, but every few steps there's a checkpoint. They're everywhere, woven into the social landscape. To continue on your way you have to pass the checkpoint. What's being controlled is right of passage – access. It's about your enablement to go places and do things. When you pass the checkpoint you have to present something for detection, and when you do that something registers. Your bank account is debited, and you and your groceries pass. Or something fails to register, and that's what lets you pass, like at airport security or places where there's video surveillance. In either case what's being controlled is passage across thresholds.

Society becomes an open field composed of thresholds or gateways, it becomes a continuous space of passage. It's no longer rigidly structured by walled-in enclosures, there's all kinds of latitude. It's just that at key points along the way, at key thresholds, power is tripped into action. The exercise of the power bears on your movement – not so much you as a person. In the old disciplinary power formations, it was always about judging what sort of person you were, and the way power functioned was to make you fit a model, or else. If you weren't the model citizen, you were judged guilty and locked up as a candidate for 'reform'. That kind of power deals with big unities – the person as moral subject, right and wrong, social order. And everything was internalized – if you didn't think right you were in trouble. Now you're checked in passing, and instead of being judged innocent or guilty you're registered as liquid. The process is largely automatic, and it doesn't really matter what you think or who you are deep down. Machines do the detecting and 'judging'. The check just bears on a little detail – do you have enough in your bank account, do you not have a gun? It's a highly localized, partial exercise of power – a micro-power. That micropower, though, feeds up to higher levels, bottom up.

Mary Zournazi: And this power is more intangible because it has no 'real' origin...

Brian Massumi: In a way the real power starts after you've passed, in the feed, because you've left a trace. Something has registered. Those registrations can be gathered to piece together a profile of your movement, or they can be compared to other people's inputs. They can be processed en masse and systematized, synthesized. Very convenient for surveillance or crime investigation, but even more valuable for marketing. In such a fluid economy, based so much on intangibles, the most valuable thing is information on people's patterns and tastes. The checkpoint system allows information to be gathered at every step you take. You're providing a continuous feed, which comes back to you in advertising pushing new products, new bundlings of potential. Think of how cookies work on the internet. Every time you click a link, you're registering your tastes and patterns, which are then processed and thrown back at you in the form of flip-up ads that try to get you to go to particular links and hopefully buy something. It's a feedback loop, and the object is to modulate your online movement. It's no exaggeration to say that every time you click a link you're doing somebody else's market research for them. You're contributing to their profit-making abilities. Your everyday movements and leisure activities have become a form of value-producing labour. You are generating surplus-value just by going about your daily life – your very ability to move is being capitalized on. Deleuze and Guattari call this kind of capitalizing on movement 'surplus-value of flow', and what characterizes the 'society of control' is that the economy and the way power functions come together around the generation of this surplus-value of flow. Life movements, capital and power become one continuous operation – check, register, feed-in, processing, feedback, purchase, profit, around and around.

Mary Zournazi: So how do the more 'traditional' forms of power operate? I mean they don't disappear – they seem to gather more momentum?

Brian Massumi: Yes, this situation doesn't mean that police functions and the other old disciplinary forms of power are over and done with. Disciplinary powers don't disappear. Far from it. In fact they tend to proliferate and often get more vehement in their application precisely because the field that they are in is no longer controlled overall by their kind of power, so they're in a situation of structural insecurity. There are no more top-down state apparatuses that can really claim effective control over their territory. Old-style sovereignty is a thing of the past. All borders have become porous, and capitalism is feeding off that poracity and pushing it further and further – that's what globalization is all about. But there have to be mechanisms that check those movements, so policing functions start to proliferate, and as policing proliferates so do prisons. In the US they're being privatized and are now big business. Now policing works more and more in the way I was just describing, through gatekeeping – detection, registration and feedback. Police action, in the sense of an arrest, comes out of this movement-processing loop as a particular kind of feedback. Instead of passing through the gate, a gun is detected by the machine, and a police response is triggered, and someone gets arrested. Police power becomes a function of that other kind of power, that we were calling control, or movement-based power. It's a local stop-action that arises out of the flow and is aimed at safeguarding it. The boom in prison construction comes as an offshoot of the policing, so you could consider the profits made by that new industry as a kind of surplus-value of flow. It's a vicious circle, and everyone knows it. No matter how many prisons there are, no matter how many people they lock up, the general insecurity won't be lessened. It just comes with the territory, because for capitalism to keep going, things have to keep flowing. Free trade and fluidity of labour markets is the name of the game. So no matter how many billions of dollars are poured into surveillance and prison building, the threat will still be there of something getting through that shouldn't. Terrorism is the perfect example.

Mary Zournazi: Yes. In thinking about this now – after our initial conversation and in this revision of it, post-September 11 – it adds another dimension to this surveillance.

Brian Massumi: All the September 11 terrorists were in the US legally. They passed. How many others might have? With this stage of capitalism comes territorial insecurity, and with territorial insecurity comes fear, with fear comes more checkpoint policing, more processing, more bottom-up, fed-back 'control'. It becomes one big, self-propelling feedback machine. It turns into a kind of automatism, and we register collectively as individuals through the way we feed that automatism, by our participation in it, just by virtue of being alive and moving. Socially, that's what the individual is now: a checkpoint trigger and a co-producer of surplus-values of flow. Power is now distributed. It trickles down to the most local, most partial checkpoint. The profits that get generated from that don't necessarily trickle down, but the power does. There is no distance any more between us, our movements and the operations of power, or between the operations of power and the forces of capitalism. One big, continuous operation. Capitalist power has become operationalized. Nothing so glorious as sovereign, just operational – a new modesty of power as it becomes ubiquitous.

At any rate, the hope that might come with the feeling of potentialization and enablement we discussed is doubled by insecurity and fear. Increasingly power functions by manipulating that affective dimension rather than dictating proper or normal behaviour from on high. So power is no longer fundamentally normative, like it was in its disciplinary forms, it's affective. The media have an extremely important role to play in that. The legitimization of political power, of state power, no longer goes through the reason of state and the correct application of governmental judgement. It goes through affective channels. For example, an American president can deploy troops overseas because it makes a population feel good about their country or feel secure, not because the leader is able to present well-honed arguments that convince the population that it is a justified use of force. So there is no longer political justification within a moral framework provided by the sovereign state. And the media are not mediating any more – they become direct mechanisms of control by their ability to modulate the affective dimension.

This has all become painfully apparent after the World Trade Center attacks. You had to wait weeks after the event to hear the slightest analysis in the US media. It was all heart-rending human interest stories of fallen heroes, or scare stories about terrorists around every corner. What the media produced wasn't information or analysis – it was affect modulation, affective pick-up from the mythical 'man in the street', followed by affective amplification through broadcast and diffusion. Another feedback loop. It changes how people experience what potentials they have to go and to do. The constant security concerns insinuate themselves into our lives at such a basic, habitual level that you're barely aware how it's changing the tenor of everyday living. You start 'instinctively' to limit your movements and contact with people. It's affectively limiting. That affective limitation is expressed in emotional terms – remember we were making a distinction between affect and emotion, with emotion being the expression of affect in gesture and language, its conventional or coded expression. At the same time as the media helps produce this affective limitation, it works to overcome it in a certain way. The limitation can't go too far or it would slow down the dynamic of capitalism. One of the biggest fears after September 11 was that the economy would go into recession because of a crisis in consumer confidence. So everyone was called upon to keep spending, as a proud, patriotic act. So the media picks up on fear and insecurity and feeds it back amplified, but in a way that somehow changes its quality into pride and patriotism – with the proof in the purchasing. A direct affective conversion of fear into confidence by means of an automatic image loop, running in real time, through continuous coverage, and spinning off profit. Does anyone really believe Bush stands for state reason? It doesn't matter – there are flags to wave and feel-good shopping to do. Once the loop gets going, you've got to feed it. You can only produce more pride and patriotism by producing more fear and insecurity to convert. At times it seemed as though US government officials were consciously drumming up fear, like when they repeatedly issued terrorist attack warnings and then would withdraw them – and the media was lapping it up.

Mary Zournazi: Yes.

Brian Massumi: Affect is now much more important for understanding power, even state power narrowly defined, than concepts like ideology. Direct affect modulation takes the place of old-style ideology. This is not new. It didn't just happen around the September 11 events, it just sort of came out then, became impossible to ignore. In the early 1990s I put together a book called *The Politics of Everyday Fear*.[1] It dealt with the same kind of mechanisms, but it was coming out of the experience of the 1980s, the Reagan years. This directly affective media power has been around at least since television matured as a medium – which was about when it took power literally, with the election of Reagan, an old TV personality, as head of state. The functions of head of state and commander-in-chief of the military fused with the role of the television personality. The American president was not a statesman any more, like Woodrow Wilson or Franklin Roosevelt were. He was a visible personification of that affective media loop. The face of mass affect. Now, the internet is taking up where television left off. With the internet, the affective conversion loops becomes more diffuse and distributed – and all the more insidious. What was once mass affect has now entered into the micropolitical realm, where it proliferates. This allows it to mutate more readily into new variations, but also for some of those variations to spike virally.

Mary Zournazi: It is really important to understand affect 'after a society of ideology'. Ideology is still around but it is not as embracing as it was, and in fact it does operate. But to really understand it you have to understand its materialization, which goes through

---

[1] Brian Massumi, ed., *The Politics of Everyday Fear* (Minneapolis: University of Minnesota Press, 1993).

affect. That's a very different way of addressing the political, because it is having to say that there is a whole range of ideological structures in place. Then there is that point you were talking about, the transitional passages that you pass through that capitalism is part of and manipulating – but it does have the possibility of freedom within it. It seems to me that to express how those affective dimensions are mobilized is the main ethical concern now...

Brian Massumi: It seems to me that alternative political action does not have to fight against the idea that power has become affective, but rather has to learn to function itself on that same level – meet affective modulation with affective modulation. That requires, in some ways, a performative, theatrical or aesthetic approach to politics. For example, it is not possible for a dispossessed group to adequately communicate its needs and desires through the usual channels. It just doesn't happen. It wasn't possible for marginal interest groups like the anti-globalization movement before the Seattle demonstration (1999) to do that simply by arguing convincingly and broadcasting its message. The message doesn't get through, because the public discourse doesn't function on that level of the rational weighing of choices. Unfortunately the kind of theatrical or performative intervention that is the easiest and has the most immediate effect is often a violent kind. If windows hadn't been broken and cars hadn't been overturned in Seattle, most people wouldn't have heard of the anti-globalization movement by now. That outburst of anger actually helped create networks of people working around the world trying to address the increasing inequalities that accompany globalization. It was able to shake the situation enough that people took notice. It was like everything was thrown up in the air for a moment and people came down after the shock in a slightly different order and some were interconnected in ways that they hadn't been before. Dispossessed people like the Palestinians or the people in Irian Jaya just can't argue their cases effectively through the media, which is why they're sometimes driven to violent guerrilla tactics or terrorism, out of desperation. And they're basically theatrical or spectacular actions, they're performative, because they don't do much in themselves except to get people's attention – and cause a lot of suffering in the process, which is why they spectacularly backfire as often as not. They also work by amplifying fear on all sides, which then gets converted into group pride or resolve. The resolve is for the in-group and the fear for everybody else. It's as divisive as the oppression it's responding to, and it feeds right into the dominant state mechanisms.

The September 11 terrorists made Bush president, they created President Bush, they fed the massive military and surveillance machine he's now able to build. Before Bin Laden and al-Qaeda, Bush wasn't a president, he was an embarrassment. Bin Laden and Bush are affective partners, like Bush Senior and Saddam Hussein, or Reagan and the Soviet leaders. In a way, they're in collusion or in symbiosis. They're like evil twins who feed off of each other's affective energies. It's a kind of vampiric politics. Everything starts happening between these opposite personifications of affect, leaving no room for other kinds of action. It's rare that protest violence has the kind of positive organizing power it did in Seattle. The anti-globalization movement had already lost that power by the time it reached Genoa (2001), when people started to die. The violence was overused by certain elements of the movement and under-strategized – it got predictable, it became a refrain, it lost its power.

The crucial political question for me is whether there are ways of practising a politics that takes stock of the affective way power operates now, but doesn't rely on violence and the hardening of divisions along identity lines that it usually brings. I'm not exactly sure what that kind of politics would look like, but it would still be performative, and it would resist personification in peak individuals. In some basic way it would be an aesthetic politics, because its aim would be to expand the range of affective potential – which is what aesthetic practice has always been about. It's also the way I talked about ethics earlier. Félix Guattari liked to hyphenate the two – towards an 'ethico-aesthetic politics'.

Mary Zournazi: For me the relationship you were discussing earlier, between hope and fear in the political domain, is what gets mobilized by the Left and Right. In some ways the problem of more leftist or radical thinking is that it doesn't actually tap into those mobilizations of different kinds of affects, whether it be hope, fear, love or whatever. The Left are criticizing the Right and the Right are mobilizing hope and fear in more affective ways. The Right can capture the imagination of a population and produce nationalist feelings and tendencies, so there can be a real absence of hope to counter what's going on in everyday life, and I think the Left have a few more hurdles to jump...

Brian Massumi: The traditional Left was really left behind by the culturalization or socialization of capital and the new functioning of the mass media. It seems to me that in the United States what's left of the Left has become extremely isolated. So there is a sense of hopelessness and isolation that ends up rigidifying people's responses. They're left to stew in their own righteous juices. They risk falling back on rectitude and right judgement, which simply is not affective. Or rather, it's anti-affective affect – it's curtailing, punishing, disciplining. When this happens, it's really just a sad holdover from the old regime – the dregs of disciplinary power. It seems to me that the Left has to relearn resistance, really taking to heart the changes that have happened recently in the way capitalism and power operate, and learning from the successes and failures of the anti-globalization movement.

Mary Zournazi: In a way, this conversation makes me think about the relation of 'autonomy and connection' that you've written about. There are many ways of understanding autonomy, but I think with capitalism's changing face it is harder and harder to be autonomous. For instance, people who are unemployed have very intense reactions and feelings to that categorization of themselves as unemployed. And, in my experience, I'm continually hounded by bureaucratic procedures that tend to restrict my autonomy and freedom – such as constant checks, meetings and forms to fill out. These procedures mark every step you take...So to find some way to affirm unemployment that allows you to create another life, or even to get a job, is increasingly more difficult and produces new forms of alienation and 'disconnection'...

Brian Massumi: It is harder to feel like getting a job is making you autonomous, because there are so many mechanisms of control that come down on you when you do have a job. All aspects of your life involve these mechanisms – your daily schedules, your dress, and, in the United States, it can even involve such invasive procedures as being tested for drugs on a regular basis. Even when you are not on the job, the insecurity that goes with having a job and wanting to keep it in a volatile economy – where there is little job security and the kind of jobs that are available change very quickly – requires you to constantly be thinking of your marketability and what the next job is going to be. So free time starts getting taken up by self-improvement or taking care of yourself so that you remain healthy and alert and can perform at your peak. The difference between your job life and off-job life collapses, there are no longer distinctions between your public and private functions. Being unemployed creates an entirely different set of challenges, constraints and controls, but it is not necessarily completely disempowering. For example, a lot of creative work gets done by people who are unemployed or underemployed.

Mary Zournazi: Yes, but it is also the intensity of those experiences that get categorized in one particular way

– you either work or don't work. But the way it's lived out isn't like that at all. I'm not just thinking of myself here and my experience of unemployment. The feeling of despair doesn't have a way of being expressed in our cultures, except with the feeling that you're not doing the right thing, or you're not part of the society. It is about the relationship to commodities, really, because in a sense you are no longer in a position to market yourself or consume.

Brian Massumi: There is definitely an imperative to have a job and to be able to consume more and consume better, to consume experiences that in-form you and increase your marketability for jobs. There's definitely an imperative to participate, and if you can't you're branded, you don't pass any more, you can't get by the most desirable checkpoints.

Mary Zournazi: Yes, like getting a credit card – or simply having money in your bank account.

Brian Massumi: But what I was trying to say is that there is no such thing as autonomy and decisive control over one's life in any total sense, whether you have a job or whether you don't. There are different sets of constraints, and, like we were saying before, freedom always arises from constraint – it's a creative conversion of it, not some utopian escape from it. Wherever you are, there is still potential, there are openings, and the openings are in the grey areas, in the blur where you're susceptible to affective contagion, or capable of spreading it. It's never totally within your personal power to decide.

Mary Zournazi: Is that what you mean by autonomy and connection?

Brian Massumi: Well, there's no such thing as autonomy in the sense of being entirely affectively separate. When you are unemployed you are branded as separate, unproductive and not part of society, but you still are connected because you are in touch with an enormous range of social services and policing functions that mean you are just as much in society – but you are in society in a certain relation of inequality and impasse. It's a fiction that there is any position within society that enables you to maintain yourself as a separate entity with complete control over your decisions – the idea of a free agent that somehow stands back from it all and chooses, like from a smorgasbord platter. I think there can be another notion of autonomy that has to do more with how you can connect to others and to other movements, how you can modulate those connections, to multiply and intensify them. So what you are, affectively, isn't a social classification – rich or poor, employed or unemployed – it's a set of potential connections and movements that you have, as a function of those classifications, but always in an open field of relations. What you can do, your potential, is ultimately defined by your connectedness, the way you're connected and how intensely, not your ability to separate off and decide by yourself. Autonomy is always connective, it's not being apart, it's being in, being in a situation of belonging that gives you certain degrees of freedom, or powers of becoming, powers of emergence. How many degrees of freedom there are, and where they can lead most directly, is certainly different depending on how you are socially classified – whether you are male or female, child or adult, rich or poor, employed or unemployed – but none of those conditions or definitions are boxes that completely contain a person's potential. And having pity for someone who occupies a category that is not socially valorized, or expressing moral outrage on their behalf, is not necessarily what is helpful in the long run, because it maintains the category and simply inverts its value sign, from negative to positive. It's a kind of piety, a moralizing approach. It's not affectively pragmatic. It doesn't challenge identity-based divisions.

Mary Zournazi: Well, that is the problem of charity. When you have pity for someone it doesn't actually change the situation or give them much hope. But the other side of that is what you were talking about before, the idea of 'caring for belonging'. There is such a focus on self-interest and the privatized idea of the individual (although this is changing through the new fields of capitalism and the economy) – the valorization of the individual against more collective struggles. This project has been trying to think about different notions of being, and collective life. In your ideas of autonomy and connection there is also another understanding or different notion of care – 'belonging' and our 'relations' to ourselves and others. It involves some other idea of being that is anti-capitalist, and also different notion of caring...

Brian Massumi: Well, if you think of your life as an autonomous collectivity or a connective autonomy, it still makes sense to think in terms of self-interest at a certain level. Obviously a disadvantaged group has to assess its interests and fight for certain rights, certain rights of passage and access, certain resources – often survival itself is in the balance. But at the same time, if any group, disadvantaged or otherwise, identifies itself completely with its self-interests it's living the fiction that it is a separate autonomy. It is missing the potential that comes from taking the risk of making an event of the way you relate to other people, orienting it towards becoming-other. So in a way you are cutting yourself off from your own potential to change and intensify your life. If you think of it in terms of potential and intensified experience then too much self-interest is against your own interests. You have to constantly be balancing those two levels. Political actions that only operate in terms of the self-interest of identified groups occupying recognizable social categories like male/female, unemployed/employed, have limited usefulness. For me, if they are pursued to the exclusion of other forms of political activity they end up creating a sort of rigidity – a hardening of the arteries!

Mary Zournazi: Which leads to a heart attack or death, doesn't it!

Brian Massumi: So it seems to me there needs to be an ecology of practices that does have room for pursuing or defending rights based on an identification with a certain categorized social group, that asserts and defends a self-interest but doesn't just do that. If you do think of your life potential as coming from the ways you can connect with others, and are challenged by that connection in ways that might be outside your direct control, then, as you are saying, you have to employ a different kind of logic. You have to think of your being in a direct belonging. There are any number of practices that can be socially defined and assert their interest, but all of them interact in an open field. If you take them all together there is an in-betweenness of them all that is not just the one-to-one conflict between pairs, but snakes between them all and makes them belong to the same social field – an indeterminate or emergent 'sociality'. So I'm suggesting that there is a role for people who care for relation or belonging, as such, and try to direct attention towards it and inflect it rather than denouncing or championing particular identities or positions. But to do that you have to abdicate your own self-interest up to a point, and this opens you to risk. You have to place yourself not in a position but in the middle, in a fairly indeterminate, fairly vague situation, where things meet at the edges and pass into each other.

Mary Zournazi: That's the ethics, isn't it?

Brian Massumi: Yes, because you don't know what the outcome is going to be. So you have to take care, because an intervention that is too violent can create rebound effects that are unpredictable to such a degree that it can lead to things falling apart rather than reconfiguring. It can lead to great suffering. In a way I think it becomes an ethic of caring, caring for belonging, which has to be a nonviolent ethic that involves thinking of your local actions as modulating a global state. A very small intervention might get amplified across the web of connections to produce large effects – the famous butterfly effect – you never know. So it takes a great deal of attention and care and abductive effort of understanding about how things are interrelating and how a perturbation, a little shove or a tweak, might change that.

Mary Zournazi: Yes, and there is a relation between this ethics, hope and the idea of joy. If we take Spinoza and Nietzsche seriously, an ethic of joy and the cultivation of joy are an affirmation of life. In the sense of what you are saying, even a small thing can become amplified and can have a global effect, which is life-affirming. What are your thoughts on this ethical relationship in everyday existence? And in intellectual practice – which is where we are coming from – what are the affirmations of joy and hope?

Brian Massumi: Well, I think that joy is not the same thing as happiness. Just like good for Nietzsche is not the opposite of evil, joy for Spinoza (or 'gaiety' in Nietzsche's vocabulary) is not the opposite of unhappy. It's on a different axis. Joy can be very disruptive, it can even be very painful. What I think Spinoza and Nietzsche are getting at is joy as affirmation, an assuming by the body of its potentials, its assuming of a posture that intensifies its powers of existence. The moment of joy is the co-presence of those potentials, in the context of a bodily becoming. That can be an experience that overcomes you. Take Antonin Artaud, for example. His artistic practice was all about intensifying bodily poten-tial, trying to get outside or underneath the categories of language and affective containment by those catego-ries, trying to pack vast potentials for movement and meaning in a single gesture, or in words that burst apart and lose their conventional meaning, becoming like a scream of possibility, a babble of becoming, the body bursting out through an opening in expression. It's liberating, but at the same time the charge of that potential can become unbearable and can actually destroy. Artaud himself was destroyed by it, he ended up mad, and so did Nietzsche. So it is not just simple opposition between happy and unhappy or pleasant or unpleasant.

I do think, though, that the practice of joy does imply some form of belief. It can't be a total scepticism or nihilism or cynicism, which are all mechanisms for holding oneself separate and being in a position to judge, deride or disqualify. But, on the other hand, it's not a belief in the sense of a set of propositions to adhere to or a set of principles or moral dictates. There is a phrase of Deleuze's that I like very much where he says that what we need is to be able to find a way to 'believe in the world' again. It's not at all a theological statement – or an anti-theological statement for that matter. It's an ethical statement. What it is saying is that we have to live our immersion in the world, really experience our belonging to this world, which is the same thing as our belonging to each other, and live that so intensely together that there is no room to doubt the reality of it. The idea is that lived intensity is self-affirming. It doesn't need a God or judge or head of state to tell it that it has value. What it means, I think, is accept the embeddedness, go with it, live it out, and that's your reality, it's the only reality you have, and it's your participation that makes it real. That's what Deleuze is saying belief is about, a belief in the world. It's not a belief that's 'about' being in the world, it *is* a being in the world. Because it's all about being in this world, warts and all, and not some perfect world beyond or a better world of the future, it's an empirical kind of belief. Ethical, empirical – and creative, because your participation in this world is part of a global becoming. So it's about taking joy in that process, wherever it leads, and I guess it's about having a kind of faith in the world which is simply the hope that it continue...But again it is not a hope that has a particular content or end point – it's a desire for more life, or for more to life.

2

Of microperception and micropolitics

Joel McKim*: The notion of affect has become a key concept in a whole range of current discussions from questions of immaterial labour to theories of new media reception. It's a concept that obviously takes many different forms. Can you explain the particular role that affect plays within your thought?

Brian Massumi: The notion of affect does take many forms, and you're right to begin by emphasizing that. To get anywhere with the concept, you have to retain the manyness of its forms. It's not something that can be reduced to one thing. Mainly because it's not a thing. It's an event, or a dimension of every event. What interests me in the concept is that if you approach it

* Interview by Joel McKim (2008)

47

respecting its variety, you are presented with a field of questioning, a problematic field, where the customary divisions that questions about subjectivity, becoming or the political are usually couched in do not apply. My starting point is the basic Spinozan definition of affect, which is an 'ability to affect or be affected'. Right off the bat, this cuts transversally across a persistent division, probably *the* most persistent division. Because the ability to affect and the ability to be affected are two facets of the same event. One face is turned towards what you might be tempted to isolate as an object, the other towards what you might isolate as a subject. Here, they are two sides of the same coin. There is an affectation, and it is happening in-between. You start with the in-betweenness. No need to detour through well-rehearsed questions of philosophical foundations in order to cobble together a unity. You start in the middle, as Deleuze always taught, with the dynamic unity of an event.

There is a second part of the Spinozan definition taken up by Deleuze that is not cited as often. It is that a power to affect and be affected governs a transition, where a body passes from one state of capacitation to a diminished or augmented state of capacitation. This comes with the corollary that the transition is *felt*. A distinction is asserted between two levels, one of which is feeling and the other capacitation or activation. But the distinction comes in the form of a connection. This separation-connection between feeling and activation situates the account between what we would normally think of as the self on the one hand and the body on the other, in the unrolling of an event that's a becoming of the two together.

This already yields a number of terms that can be put to use and developed. First, the feeling of the transition as the body moves from one power of existence to another has a certain separability from the event it is bound up with, by virtue of its distinction from the capacitation activating the passage. What is felt is the *quality* of the experience. The account of affect will then have to directly address forms of experience, forms of life, on a qualitative register. Second, the felt transition leaves a trace, it constitutes a memory. Consequently, it can't be restricted to that one occurrence. It will return. It has already returned, in some capacity. It was already part of a series of repetitions, to the extent that the body has a past that follows it.

That's the third point: the capacitation of the body as it's gearing up for a passage towards a diminished or augmented state is completely bound up with the lived past of the body. That past includes what we think of as subjective elements, such as habits, acquired skills, inclinations, desires, even willings, all of which come in patterns of repetition. This doesn't make the event any less rooted in the body. The past that the body carries forward in serial fashion includes levels we think of as physical and biological, such as genetic inheritance and phylogenesis. So there's a reactivation of the past in passage towards a changed future, cutting transversally across dimensions of time, between past and future, and between pasts of different orders. This in-between time or transversal time is the time of the event. This temporality enables, and requires you, to rethink all of these terms – bodily capacitation, felt transition, quality of lived experience, memory, repetition, seriation, inclination – in dynamic relation to each other.

If there is one key term, that's it: relation. When you start in-between, what you're in the middle of is a region of relation. Occurrent relation, because it's all about event. Putting the terms together, you realize straight away that the relational event will play out differently every time. In repeating, it takes up the past differently. In taking up the past differently, it creates new potentials for the future. The region of occurrent relation is a point of potentiation. It is where things begin anew. Where things begin anew is where they were already present in tendency.

If there are two key terms, tendency comes next. The patterns of movement through these affective transitions are weighted for a particular body or particular situations, as more or less accessible, more or less ready to go. There's an activation not only of the body, but of the body's tendencies, as they move into and through situations. In taking account of this, you get a relational complex, a nexus, rather than a particular definition. The base definition – to affect and be affected, in a felt passage to a varied power of existence – opens a problematic field rather than ending in a particular solution. You are left with a matrix of variation that forces you to rethink the terms involved each time. You have to regenerate them to use them. It's not a general definition that you can apply. It's not a structure you can presuppose. On the other hand, it's also not the case that you're starting without any presuppositions. To start in the middle is precisely not to perform a phenomenological reduction. It is to accept the challenge to regenerate your terms, and their cohesion to each other, at each repeated step in your thinking through the nexus. Rather than a definition, what you have is a proposition, less in the logical sense than in the sense of an invitation. Starting from affect in this way is an invitation for an indefinitely constructive thinking of embodied, relational becoming. The emphasis on embodiment, variation and relation gives it an immediately political aspect that also attracted me.

Joel McKim: There are two things in your description that stand out to me as being very useful additions to the version of Spinoza's affect that is often referred to, usually via Deleuze. One is this immediately intersubjective element that seems to bring back into the picture Spinoza's idea of 'common notions' – agreements between bodies that allow the power of the individual body to be enhanced through the forming of relations. The other interesting addition you make is to include a notion of memory. You suggest that an affective experience, or the feeling of the transition from one power of existence to another, can somehow be reactivated in different series, in different relations. When you say that this memory is housed in the body, you're not necessarily speaking about an individual body, you're speaking about bodies of relations, of complexes. What happens when we move into a new set of relations? Do we start from scratch or can we bring that affective memory with us?

Brian Massumi: I think there is no such thing as starting from scratch. Everything re-begins, in a very crowded, overpopulated world. Even one body alone is pre-populated – by instincts, by inclinations, by teeming feelings and masses of memories, conscious and non-conscious, with all manner of shadings in between. The question is always 'how': how to move that crowding into a new constitution, the constitution of a becoming. Calling affect, or that felt moment of bodily moving on, calling that intersubjective is misleading if intersubjective is taken to mean that we start from a world in which there are already subjects that are preconstituted, or a pregiven structure of subject positions ready for subjects to come occupy. What is in question is precisely the emergence of the subject, its primary constitution, or its re-emergence and reconstitution. The subject of an experience emerges from a field of conditions which are not that subject yet, where it is just coming into itself. Those conditions are not yet necessarily even subjective in any normal sense. Before the subject, there's an in-mixing, a field of budding relation too crowded and heterogeneous to call intersubjective. It's not at a level where things have settled into categories like subject and object. It's the level of what William James called pure experience. When I say that it all comes back to the body, I don't mean the body as a thing apart from the self or subject. I mean that the body *is* that region of in-mixing from which subjectivity emerges. It is the coming together of the world, for experience, in a here-and-now prior to any possibility of assigning categories like subject or object. That affective region we were talking about is not in-between in the intersubjective sense. And it's not intentional in the sense of already carrying a subject–object polarity. It's a brewing, the world stirring, what I call 'bare activity'. It's a coming event, through which such categories will return – and more. Their rearising, and what else comes with them, depends on the event. It's not the event that depends on their already being in place.

———

Of *microperception and micropolitics*

Joel McKim: Then what precedes the event? What gives rise to it?

Brian Massumi: Shock. That's what Peirce says. Affect for me is inseparable from the concept of shock. It doesn't have to be a drama, though. It's really more about microshocks, the kind that populate every moment of our lives. For example a change in focus, or a rustle at the periphery of vision that draws the gaze towards it. In every shift of attention, there is an interruption, a momentary cut in the mode of onward deployment of life. The cut can pass unnoticed, striking imperceptibly, with only its effects entering conscious awareness as they unroll. This is the onset of the activation I was referring to earlier. I'd go so far as to say that this onset of experience is by nature imperceptible.

This is one way of understanding 'microperception', a concept of great importance to Deleuze and Guattari. Microperception is not smaller perception, it's a perception of a qualitatively different kind. It's something that is felt without registering consciously. It registers only in its effects. According to this notion of shock, there is always a commotion under way, a 'something doing' as James would say. There is always a something-doing cutting in, interrupting whatever continuities are in progress. For things to continue, they have to re-continue. They have to re-jig around the interruption. At the instant of re-jigging, the body braces for what will come. It in-braces, in the sense that it returns to its potential for more of life to come, and that potential is immanent to its own arising.

You can sometimes feel the in-bracing itself, most noticeably in startles or frights. Before you can even

consciously recognize what you're afraid of, or even feel
that it is yourself that is the subject of the feeling, you
are catapulted into a feeling of the frightfulness of the
situation. It only dawns on you in the next instant that
you'd better figure out what might have done the cata-
pulting, and what you should do about it. It is only then
that you own the feeling as your own, and recognize it
as a content of your life, an emotional episode in your
personal history. But in the instant of the affective hit,
there is no content yet. All there is is the affective
quality, coinciding with the feeling of the interruption,
with the kind of felt transition I talked about before.
That affective quality is all there is to the world in that
instant. It takes over life, fills the world, for an immeasurable instant of shock. Microperception is this purely
affective re-beginning of the world.

Microperception is bodily. There is no fright, or any
affect for that matter, without an accompanying movement in or of the body. This is the famous James–Lange
thesis. In fact, the thesis goes further, so far as to say
that this bodily commotion is what an emotion *is*. James
calls it emotion, but at the generative level it is what
we're calling affect. The James–Lange thesis has been
widely criticized as reductive, but this is to misunder-
stand it. Because the body, in this eventful re-beginning,
carries tendencies reviving the past and already striving
towards a future. In its commotion are capacities reactivating, being primed to play out, in a heightening or
diminishing of their collective power of existence. The
body figures here as a cut in the continuity of relation,
filled with potential for re-relating, with a difference.
Microperceptual shock is like a re-cueing of our bodily
powers of existence. Here, the body is what Peirce calls

a 'material quality': a coming quality of experience that is being actively lived-in before it's actually lived out. It's lived-in in intensity, in a kind of existential agitation, a poising or posturing for the coming event, a kind of recoil, not to withdraw from the world, but rather to brace for it again, and for how else it will be.

The world in which we live is literally made of these reinaugural microperceptions, cutting in, cueing emergence, priming capacities. Every body is at every instant in thrall to any number of them. A body is a complex of in-bracings playing out complexly and in serial fashion. The tendencies and capacities activated do not necessarily bear fruit. Some will be summoned to the verge of unfolding, only to be left behind, unactualized. But even these will have left their trace. In that moment of interruptive commotion, there's a productive indecision. There's a constructive suspense. Potentials resonate and interfere, and this modulates what actually eventuates. Even what doesn't happen has a modulatory effect. Whitehead had a word for this. He called it 'negative prehension'. It's a somewhat paradoxical concept. It refers to an unfelt feeling entering positively into the constitution of an experience by dint of its active exclusion from it. The concept of affect is tied to the idea of modulation occurring at a constitutive level where many somethings are doing, most of them unfelt. Or again, felt only in effect. No less real for passing unfelt.

Say there are a number of bodies indexed to the same cut, primed to the same cue, shocked in concert. What happens is a collective event. It's distributed across those bodies. Since each body will carry a different set of tendencies and capacities, there is no guarantee that they will act in unison even if they are cued in concert. However different their eventual actions, all will have unfolded from the same suspense. They will have been attuned – differentially – to the same interruptive commotion. 'Affective attunement' – a concept from Daniel Stern – is a crucial piece in the affective puzzle.[1] It is a way of approaching affective politics that is much more supple than notions more present in the literature of what's being called the 'affective turn', like imitation or contagion, because it finds difference in unison, and concertation in difference. Because of that, it can better reflect the complexity of collective situations, as well as the variability that can eventuate from what might be considered the 'same' affect. There is no sameness of affect. There is affective difference in the same event. Reactions to fear, to turn to that classic example again, vary wildly, and even vary significantly at different times in the same individual's life.

Joel McKim: You mention the notion of affective politics. Can you speak more about the way in which this manner of thinking about events and microperceptions is political?

Brian Massumi: Politics, approached affectively, is an art of emitting the interruptive signs, triggering the cues, that attune bodies while activating their capacities differentially. Affective politics is inductive. Bodies can be

[1] Daniel Stern, *The Interpersonal World of the Infant: A View from Psychoanalysis and Developmental Psychology* (New York: Basic Books, 1985), pp. 138–61.

inducted into, or attuned to, certain regions of tendency, futurity and potential, they can be induced into inhabiting the same affective environment, even if there is no assurance they will act alike in that environment. A good example is an alarm, a sign of threat or danger. Even if you conclude in the next instant that it's a false alarm, you will have come to that conclusion in an environment that is effectively one of threat. Others who have heard the alarm may well respond differently, but they will be responding differently together, as inhabitants of the same affective environment. Everyone registering the alarm will have been attuned to the same threat event, in one way or another. It is the sum total of the different ways of being interpellated by the same event that will define what it will have been politically. The event can't be fully predetermined. It will be as it happens. For there to be uniformity of response, other factors must have been active to pre-channel tendencies. Politics of conformity pivoting on the signalling of threat, like the politics that held sway during the Bush administration, must work on many levels and at many rhythms of bodily priming to ensure a relative success. And again, there will be minor lines that won't be emphasized or come out into relief or be fully enacted but that everyone will have felt in that unfeeling way of negatively prehending. Those are left as a reservoir of political potential. It is a potential that is immediately collective. It's not a mere possibility, it's an active part of the constitution of that situation, it's just one that hasn't been fully developed, that hasn't been fully capacitated for unfolding. This means that there are potential alter-politics at the collectively in-braced heart of every situation, even the most successfully conformist in its mode of attunement. You can return to that reservoir of real but unexpressed potential, and re-cue it. This would be a politics of microperception: a micropolitics. The Obama campaign's re-cueing of fear towards hope might be seen as targeting that micropolitical level, interestingly, through macro-media means.

Even in the most controlled political situation, there's a surplus of unacted-out potential that is collectively felt. If cued into, it can remodulate the situation. As Deleuze and Guattari liked to say, there is no ideology and never was. What they mean by that is no situation is ever fully predetermined by ideological structures or codings. Any account paying exclusive attention to that level is fatally incomplete. No situation simply translates ideological inculcations into action. There's always an event, and the event always includes dimensions that aren't completely actualized, so it's always open to a degree, it's always dynamic and in re-formation. To be in effect, ideological predeterminations have to enter the event and *take* effect. They have to reassert themselves, to make themselves effectively ingredient to the event. Their effectiveness is always an accomplishment, a renewed victory, and what needs to be accomplished can fail. Micropolitics, affective politics, seeks the degrees of openness of any situation, in hopes of priming an alter-accomplishment. Just modulating a situation in a way that amplifies a previously unfelt potential to the point of perceptibility is an alter-accomplishment.

Joel McKim: And the question of memory? Can that qualitative change, or change in affective tonality, be remembered and brought into a different context? Can it be transported?

Of microperception and micropolitics

Brian Massumi: There are different kinds of memory. There's a kind of memory that's directly implicated in any perception, couched in acquired or inbred inclinations and propensities that a body carries forward. This is a past that is not in any subjective representation, it's a past that is only in its activation. It's an enacted past, actively present. It's not in the head, but in the middle, in rearising relationship, in situation. It's as much like a thought as an action.

It's like a thought in the sense that it has a certain generality. A tendency or propensity fuses, or contracts, a great number of past occasions into a readiness for a next. A habit or a skill is acquired through repetition. But once we have contracted it, we don't have the repetitions, we have a capacity to redeploy a sequence of actions, including on-the-fly variations responding instantaneously to particularities of the situation. It's an adaptive potential unfolding for the situation. It comes into the present as an inheritance of the past, but only to the extent that it is readying a future. This kind of memory is what Whitehead calls the immediate past, because it coincides with the immediacy of the present. It's by nature nonconscious. It takes you, before you have it as your memory. It catapults you into unfolding tendency before any possibility of reflection. It might not be acted out. It might remain behind in the inaugural commotion of the coming event. It might just agitate immanently, in which case it remains what Bergson calls a 'nascent' or 'incipient' action.

On the other hand, it might well catapult you directly into action. In either case the first making of the moment, the inauguration of the event, is that absolute coincidence between the past and the dawning present. Not a subject thinking or being towards the world, but the world reconstituting itself around an actively present germ of the past. There's already, in that immeasurable instant of incipience, an activation of tendencies towards the future. The future has a kind of felt presence, an affective presence, as an attractor. Because each tendency tends towards a certain kind of outcome. It is attracted by its own end. That end point is what James calls a 'terminus'. It's a limit point governing the direction of an unfolding. Again, that's like a thought, if you can consider thinking an effective presence of what isn't actually there. By being effectively present without actually being there I don't mean being consciously projected on the future as a possibility. It's a pulling of the present, already pregnant with pastness, out of itself, from within its own event. It's a force of time acting immanently to the occurrence. It's a real, generative factor of the forming moment. I call it a force because it has a certain kind of efficacy, a formative power. I like to call this formative participation of the future 'quasi-causal', because it is more like an attractor in chaos theory than an efficient material cause. Whitehead insists that the future is also always active in the 'energizing' of the present by the past that inaugurates a coming event.

All that happens in the cut, in the instant of commotion, microshock, or welling event-suspense. It occurs on the microperceptual level, in an interval smaller than the smallest perceivable, to paraphrase Deleuze. It cannot be consciously perceived. What we perceive is what unfolds from that interpenetration of moments, as the coming event plays itself out. We perceive the trailing into the situation of the past already tending out of that situation towards the future of the event's having happened. What we experience is like a Doppler effect of the force of time. It is due to this Doppler effect that we experience the moment, that is, that we experience a duration, that we feel time to have extension. That duration is our experience straddling those dimensions of time, as much like a thought as in unfolding action. The duration registers with an affective tonality. We have a primarily qualitative experience of time extension. This qualitatively lived time is what William James called the specious present. It's 'specious' because it's all coming out of a fissure in time, a cut in time, a shock and suspense. The microshocks don't stop. They come in droves, all in intervals smaller than the smallest perceivable. All cut, all the time, in infinite division. It is only because an affective tonality envelops groupings of them, continues through or around them, that we feel the moment as having extension, rather than feeling it implode into an infinitely proliferating fractal cut. It is the quality of the experience that makes the moment, and gives it its continuity, that makes it a duration. The present is held aloft by affect. This is also something that Whitehead insists on: affect is not in time, it makes time, it makes time present, it makes the present moment, it's a creative factor in the emergence of time as we effectively experience it, it's constitutive of lived time.

Conscious memory is quite different from this kind of memory, that of the immediate past that contributes to activating the event of lived experience. Conscious memory is retrospective, going from the present to reactivate the past, whereas active memory moves in the other direction, coming from the past to energize the present. Then there's another kind of memory, a Kierkegaardian memory. Kierkegaard talks about how we 'remember forwards, but recall backwards'. Recalling backwards is conscious remembering. Remembering forwards is the feeling of the attractor, the end point or terminus, making itself felt as the limit point of a tendency contracted in the past, and now reactivated. The attractor is a futurity, but it's memory-like in that it only has futurity by virtue of contracting pastness. It pulls a contracted past through the crucible of the present, towards itself, the not-yet of this event. I think this idea of the terminus can be linked to what Whitehead calls an 'eternal object' (a misnomer if there ever was one, because it isn't an object but a potential, and it isn't eternal in the sense of enduring through time, but rather in the sense that it enters actively into the constitution of every moment).

So there are at least those three kinds of memory: a nonconscious memory of the present, which is the past actively contracted into the cut of the present instant (what I call the 'here-and-now' to differentiate it from the specious present that encompasses and unifies its fractal teeming and gives it the continuity of a duration); a memory of the past, which is a rear view of the past from the perspective of the consciously experienced specious present of lived duration; and a felt memory of the future, which is the quasi-causal force of tendency taking effect, governed recursively by the futurity of the terminus towards which it tends. All of these forms of memory can operate at the same time, and in our waking lives they usually do. They are complements of each other.

Of microperception and micropolitics

For the question of whether the qualitative change registering in affective tonality is transportable, the answer would have to be no, not strictly speaking. All the things we have talked about are generative factors of an event. Affect is one creative factor entering into the constitution of events, even if it is a very special one. It is not a content that can be transported from one event to another. Like all event-factors, it can be repeated, reactivated, it can rearise, but always anew. The logic of affect is entirely bound up with the logic of serial repetition and difference that applies to events. It's an event-logic, not a logic of transmission or communication.

Joel McKim: Part of what made me interested in unfolding a little bit these different variations of memory is a notion you brought forward at the beginning of your comments, the idea that the affective shift into a different power of being carries with it a memory. A memory that also then becomes potentially reactivated or could change the experience of the body in another situation. You mentioned that these shocks occur at a microperceptual level and that there's an after-the-fact conscious duration that we experience and we hold with us that is actually quite different than the original microperceptual shock experience. Could the memory that this affective qualitative change carries with it be described as a becoming sensitive to those microperceptual shocks? So can we begin to become more aware of these affective shocks that are obviously influencing us or having an impact on us continuously? Is that part of the potential process?

63

Brian Massumi: Yes, that's definitely part of the potential process. It's a way of acquiring new propensities, which if they become embedded in our everyday life are habits. As they repeat themselves, we become aware *that* they function, even if we are not aware of them *as* they function. That secondary awareness easily wears out. Habits are ways of not attending-to, while still acting according-to. Their nonconscious functioning is self-repeating, an iterative process that can end up becoming a caricature of itself. A habit can habituate to itself. By that I meant that it can end up not attending to the newness or difference in the situations triggering it. When this happens, it has a tendency to make the coming event conform to past events. It loses its powers of adaptation, its power to renew itself, becoming a mere reflex.

The opposite can also happen. Habit can rebecome a creative force for the acquisition of new propensities, because it makes capacities available for enaction, and something can vary in the course of that making-available, and then be added to a body's repertory. To mobilize habit in this rebecoming way, the body, as you say, has to become sensitive to what's coming. It has to feel the priming, as a formative force, before it bears fruit. Perversely, this is a kind of pre-emptive power. It is a pre-emptive power that is creative of a moreness to life, what I call an ontopower. I say it's perverse because I am convinced that it is the same power mobilized by the contemporary military machine. In some of the most affect- and perception-savvy recent texts in military theory, they call this rebecoming-creative of habit 'non-recognition-based priming' and 'sampling the future'. It's part of a colonization of the mico-perceptual by the war-machine that deserves serious study.[2]

In speaking at this level, we have to be careful. If we say, 'I contract habits and then habits rule me', or 'We can remobilize habit for futurity', we are positing a subject, us or me, prior to and separate from the process of event-formation that habit is so central to. 'I' do not contract habits. Habits contract to form me. That's taking 'me' to be the relational matrix of reactivation that my body carries forward – which *is* my body as I defined it before. 'My' comes before 'me'. Leibniz insisted that being is in the possessive, not the first person. My comes before me; repetition comes before identity. And repeated difference, Deleuze adds, always trumps identity.

Joel McKim: So, shock mastery is not what we're after.

Brian Massumi: Shock mastery is not at all what we're after, I don't think. How can 'we' master what forms us? And re-forms us at each instant, before we know it? But that is not to say that we're impotent before ontopower. Quite the contrary, our lives are capacitated by it. We live it, the power of existence that we are expresses it.

Joel McKim: How do you respond to the criticism that's been widely held since critical theory that affective politics is inherently fascistic?

---

[2] See Brian Massumi, *Ontopower: War, Powers, and the State of Perception* (Durham, NC: Duke University Press, 2015).

Of *microperception and micropolitics*

Brian Massumi: I agree that the potential is there, but I don't agree that it's inherent to affective politics. The mistrust of affect seems to come from seeing affect as a primitive stimulus–response system. I connect it instead to 'priming', which does not have the linear cause–effect structure of stimulus–response, but has to do instead with modulation, which has to do with interference and resonance, which are nonlinear. Stimulus–response is a limit case. It's that case of a habit that has become a reflex, lost its adaptive power, its powers of variation, its force of futurity, that has ceased to be the slightest bit surprised by the world. It's a tired habit that has come as close to being an efficient cause as a power of repetition can get. It has let go of the 'quasi' in its causality. There is also a sense in the critiques of affective politics as fascist that nonconscious process is an absence of thought. I follow Deleuze and Guattari in saying that nonconscious process is the birth of thought. It is germinal thought, moved by the force of time to express powers of existence in coming action.

From the critical theory point of view, I just compound the sin, because I think that advocating affective politics is advocating aesthetic politics. Aesthetic politics is often also thought to be synonymous with fascism. I think about the connection between affective politics and aesthetic politics in terms of Whitehead's idea of 'contrast'. Contrasts are tendential unfoldings that are held together in the same situation. They are alternative termini that come together in the instant, even though their actual unfoldings are mutually exclusive. Their mutual exclusiveness is a kind of creative tension. It is the contrasts between termini that interfere and resonate, and modulate what comes. The specious present is the drop of experience that is one with that unfolding. It is the feeling of the resolution of the tension, as the event plays itself out, for the process to then start all over again. If thought is the effective presence of what is not actually present, a terminus is an element of thought. Then multiple termini together are an intensification of thought. The specious present feels this intensity of thinking pass into action. Normally the intensity itself is overshadowed by the effectiveness of the action it passes into. Whitehead defines the aesthetic in terms of this intensity of contrasts. An aesthetic act brings this contrastive intensity out from under the shadow of action's instrumentality or functional aim. It brings the contrastive intensity of active potential into the specious present as such, to stand alone, with no other value than itself. The aesthetic act extends the creative tension of contrast that characterizes the emergence of every action. It prolongs the suspension of the cut, the commotion of interference and resonance, gives it duration, so that it passes the threshold of perceptibility and is consciously felt as potential. This prevents the terminus from being an automatic feed forward to the end, like a reflex response to a stimulus. Resolution is suspended. The termini in play remain virtual ends. Their mutual exclusivity is still informing the situation, contributing to what it might be, but the tension doesn't have to resolve itself to be consciously felt and thought. Aesthetic politics is irresolute. It's the thinking-feeling of the virtual incompletion of definitive action.

Joel McKim: I can see the importance of this idea of an 'intensity of contrasts' for understanding processes of creativity and invention, but in what way precisely is this political?

Brian Massumi: It might not sound political, at least in the way it's usually meant. But it is, because the virtuality is of an event to come, and as we saw before, the event always has the potential to affectively attune a multiplicity of bodies to its happening, differentially. Aesthetic politics brings the collectivity of shared events to the fore, as differential, multiple, bodily potential for what might come. Difference is built into this account. Affective politics, understood as aesthetic politics, is dissensual, in the sense that it holds contrasting alternatives together without immediately demanding that one alternative eventuate and the others evaporate. It makes thought-felt different capacities for existence, different life potentials, different forms of life, without immediately imposing a choice between them. The political question, then, is not how to find a resolution. It's not how to impose a solution. It's how to keep the intensity in what comes next. The only way is through actual differentiation. Different lines of unfolding bring the contrast into actuality, between them. The political question is then what Isabelle Stengers calls an 'ecology of practices'. How do you tend this proliferation of differentiation? How can the lines not clash and destroy each other? How do they live together? The 'solution' is not to resolve the tension through a choice, but to modulate it into a symbiosis. A cross-fertilization of capacitations that live out, to the fullest, the intensity of their coming together in the event, their belonging-together to the event.

Of microperception and micropolitics

Joel McKim: This notion of a shared differential is an interesting one. It's more usual to speak of collective politics in terms of commonality, such as the need for a common language.

Brian Massumi: I just don't think that the possibility of a common language exists any more, if it ever did. And if it did, I wouldn't want it. I don't think I'd be alone. That in itself uncommons it. It would have to be imposed. It would necessitate an exercise of power-over, very different from empowerment, the power-to of ontopower. I wouldn't want it because in my way of thinking it would be anaesthetic. It would be de-intensifying. It would flatten affect by standardizing response. It would put politics back on the uncreative road to reflex. Consensus is always the product of a power-over. It is an habituation to it, even if it's a soft form of it. I can't imagine a 'common language' that is not consensus building in a de-intensifying way.

The world is too complex to hold to that as a model. The fragmentation of nations into sub-communities, the accompanying increase in the number of nation-states formed from these communities, the destructuring effects of movements of capital, the way these unchained capital flows enable or force a constant movement of people, goods, ideas and information across borders – all of this has created a hyper-complex situation of flow and variation over which there's no effective oversight. There's no vantage point from which you could encompass it all, there's no shared perspective from which to find a common language or build a consensus or share a rationality. The situation is constitutively dissensual.

69

Rather than going back to the failed project of finding a common language, purpose or rationality, it would seem that the complexity of that dissensus should be the starting point for politics. Why accept as the starting point a reduction of difference, a channelling into tired habit? That's to start with defeat. Taking complexity for a starting point, broadly speaking, is what 'ecological' means. I see affective intensity and an aesthetics of varying life potential as the elements of an ecology of practices of the symbiotic kind called for by Stengers, and before her by Guattari. From this symbiotic perspective, an anti-capitalist politics begins by affirming the variability and potential for forms of life unleashed by capitalism itself. It continues the differentiation of forms of life already under way, but by other means, governed by other constellations of termini and embodying other values.

Joel McKim: We've begun a discussion of the micropolitical and maybe this is a good point to discuss some of the ways the micropolitical and a politics of affect can be materialized. One example is the creative, aesthetico-political events that you and Erin Manning are organizing through the SenseLab in Montreal. Could you speak about these?

Brian Massumi: Although the 'micro' of micropolitical is not synonymous with small, and although the modulations that might be effected at that level can be widely distributed, there is no better place to start than the local context in which you live and work every day. Macropolitical positioning operates under the illusion that there is a neutral, higher-level vantage point allowing you to stand outside and judge, while standing pure, correct and unsullied. Critique, practised in this way, does double duty. It opposes, too simplistically I would argue. But it also shields. To judge from outside is to ensconce yourself in an unassailable position. Micropolitically, critique has to come from within, in the thick of things, and that means getting your hands dirty. There is no situation of being outside situation. And no situation is subject to mastery. It is only by recognizing the bonds of complicity and the limitations that come with situation that you can succeed in modulating those constraints at the constitutive level, where they re-emerge and seriate. This is 'immanent critique'. It is active, participatory critique. For me, micropolitical action involves this kind of immanent critique that actively alters conditions of emergence. It engages becoming, rather than judging what is.

Erin and I are both professors, so the university is the day-to-day situation we start from, or more precisely the academic institution including its extended milieu of publishing, workshopping and conferencing. Erin is also in a fine arts department, so we operate between the art and academic institutions. In both cases there's an imperative to produce and create what is increasingly being called, importing corporate vocabulary, a 'deliverable' – a valorizable product, like a gallery-ready artwork or an article publishable in a standardized ('peer-reviewed') disciplinary journal. The emphasis is on packageable content for transmission. Increasingly, in this environment process itself becomes product, as when creative platforms developed by artists are seen as research contributions feeding product development for the 'culture industries'. Intellectual property is the new creativity. There are very strong pressures in this direction in Canada and elsewhere, where art has become 'research' ('research-creation' is what we call it in Canada), subject like all academic activity to productivity assessment. We wanted to see how far we could go, within the art and academic institutions, towards freeing creative and collaborative process from this tendency, while still continuing to survive within that environment, which for better or for worse is the one that feeds us – we can't deny our participation in it and our dependence on it – and which is overall is not going to change any time soon.

A lot of the impetus for what we're doing came from some very intense conversations we had with Isabelle Stengers, who explained that her criteria for a successful intellectual event was precisely that – that it be an event. That something really happens that wouldn't have happened otherwise. If heaven, according to an old Talking Heads song, is where nothing ever happens, then the conference is surely academic heaven. When was the last time you had a truly new thought at a conference? When was the last time that you saw an opinion changed by an academic discussion or debate? On the art side, the equivalent heavens are the artist's talk and the standard gallery exhibition. Isabelle also emphasized that it is not a question of 'freedom', in the sense of simply lifting constraints. Nothing happens most where there are no constraints, because then anything goes, and anything going is just nothing carried to a higher power, heaven to the nth degree. You might avoid the conference, but where does that get you if you end up with the kind of free-floating, free-associating discussion you might enjoy late at night in a dormitory room? Without constraints there are no stakes.

Our point of departure is what we call 'enabling constraints' – sets of designed constraints that are meant to create specific conditions for creative interaction where something is set to happen, but there is no pre-conceived notion of exactly what the outcome will be or should be. No deliverable. All process. We started practising what we thought of as event design, design for alternative-format art-academic events. The stakes aren't defined so much by issues or content or definable outcome. The stakes are the event happening or not, seeing what can be done to open up new ground for exploration and invention that re-energizes people and makes their lives in and around the institutions in which they function at the same time more liveable and more intense.

It was Erin who started the SenseLab, which I then joined as a collaborator. Looking at the milieus we were in and between, the art and academic institutions, we thought that there are things each side could offer the other – seeds of symbiosis. From the academic side, what could be brought into the art world is a tendency or propensity towards rigorous verbal expression. On the art side is a complementary propensity to invest in an object or system or interaction an intensity that rigorously exceeds language, at least standard denotative or referential uses of language. We wanted to bring together those two tendencies: bringing concepts to rigorous verbal expression, and intensifying perception and experience.

We set up at a community-based electronic arts institution, the Society for Art and Technology, that is located between the Montreal universities, in an urban space where Montreal's different language communities intermix, and where academics, university-based artists and community-based independent artists can come together. We tried to think of how to create events that would bring people together, not on a blank slate, not even on even ground, but rather from a creative bias, from the angle of what most moved them, what moved their work, what made it work. The first thing we did was to forbid anyone from bringing completed work. We wanted them to bring not the work, but what made the work work – the tendencies, skills, obsessions, attractions, inclinations that drove it from within. We set up a situation that for some would be interpreted as an artistic exhibition, for others as a conference. But it was neither. No one was going to show anything or deliver anything. The situation wasn't recognizable, which we knew could be disturbing and might intimidate. We had to have a certain estrangement, but that wasn't the point. It was just one of the enablements. We wanted to bring people together at their work's constitutive level, whereas they are used to being asked to come with it already constituted. To enable the event we had to disable certain kinds of expectations. Suspend. Like a shock, but not in the macro sense. Just enough to give pause and toggle out of default settings. We thought hard – by 'we' I mean a very dedicated collective involving students and others committed to the project – about what kinds of spatial setup would work best, how to modulate expectations as people entered the space, how to break expectations in a gentle and inviting way. We started thinking in terms of hospitality. That became our model. How do we create enabling constraints so that the situation is one of hospitality, not a test and not a show-and-tell. We tried to find very small, concrete ways of doing that, trying to anticipate the roadblocks that traditional events throw up. For instance, the moment of entry is crucial: how people enter an event implants all kinds of dynamics. Once they're in, group dynamics becomes the next challenge. Take for example the plenary. You want some whole-group interaction, otherwise the event feels dispersed and no one leaves with a sense that anything happened. But plenaries are deadly. People zone out. A few people dominate. Others don't feel empowered to speak. Discussion get too general, with the same words being used with different connotations, and no one really connecting with what anyone else is saying. It's deadly. But if you have small groups, how do you form them, and what do they do, so that they are not just plenaries in miniature? And if something really happens in a small group, which is where things are most likely to happen, how do you convey that to the other groups, or the group as a whole? These were the kinds of questions we asked.

In answer to the question of how to form small groups, we tried to find affective mechanisms. For example, in the first event we organized we had a number of pieces of fabric that were very furry and soft with beautiful colours and patterns. To divide the participants into groups, we simply asked people to pick the pieces that most attracted them, and then to use the fabric to make the space for their interaction, by sitting on it or around it or by wrapping themselves in it, whatever moved them. So before the first word was exchanged in the group or the first task begun, people were already in a little affinity-based world that had the feel of an ephemeral home. We furred them into groups. In response to the question of how to move from small groups to whole-group interaction, we laid down the enabling constraint that each group had to share, but what they had to share was their process, so that it was forbidden to report. You couldn't describe what happened, as from an outside perspective. You had to find a way to perform it again, but in a way that was adapted to the larger numbers. You couldn't report or even translate, you had to transduce. Inventing or improvising these transitions became a big part of the event. It's like the event's content was becoming its form, or vice versa. Nothing was going to happen unless everyone helped make it happen. So everybody owned the results. Everyone was actively implicated in making the event. They didn't deliver, and neither did we. Without the participants' active involvement, nothing would have happened. Since there was nothing on offer, there was nothing to be had, except what the group collectively made happen. What we were reaching for was what Guattari calls a 'subject-group'. As with all groups of that kind, what had happened wasn't immediately clear, because there was no assessable product separable from the process. What was clear at the time was only that the experience had been intense, and collective. Afterwards, things did develop: collaborations grew that had been seeded at the event. Some are still going, three years later. Processual seeds were sown that germinated on other soil. That led us to a second model, of processual dissemination, which we're still working on.

The group furring and performed transition mechanisms are little examples of what we call 'techniques of relation'. The challenge for each event is to find the enabling constraints and techniques of relation that tailor the event to what's singular about that particular coming together. To do that, you need to know something about what moves the people who will come. So there are pre-event techniques for relation that have to be in place to prepare the ground. And the post-event collaborative developments are crucial to network, because that is where what happened in the event really eventuates.

For us it's very important that what transpires be gathered in language. We're both writers. We both think of what we do as philosophy. So we always try to create a real, effective presence of philosophy. But not as a master discipline that judges other kinds of practice. We see it as a symbiosis, where practices that are not primarily linguistic are seen to bear active conceptual force that can be brought to explicit verbal expression, and by being brought into language can cycle back into the practice from which they develop to spur it further. We approach philosophy as Deleuze and Guattari define it, as the creation of concepts whose mission is to augment capacities to act, feel and perceive, in addition to think. So we approach philosophy as a creative practice in its own right, with its own material and mode of activity, which is language. Another challenge: other techniques of relation have to be invented to foster this reciprocity between different modes of creative activity and their respective materialities. A great deal of our thinking about and experimenting with event design is concerned with this, not only in our special events but in the regular day-to-day functioning of the SenseLab group, locally as well as remote, through an internet group hub.

A lot of the thinking about what we're calling techniques of relation has been done before in social movements, particularly starting in the 1960s, and in artistic movements. We have a sense that it is something that people all over the world are again feeling a hunger for, and taking up again on their own, in their own home bases, in different ways, sometimes consciously in connection with movements like the anti-globalization movement, sometimes within the smaller confines of their own institution, with a view to making it more liveable and sustaining. There is a lot of thought and experimentation going on, many techniques that have already been invented, many more on the way. We see ourselves as connecting to that wider movement, creating one more forum for that kind of activity. It's not something we feel we've invented or in any way own. It's in continuity with a discontinuous tradition – a set of practices and orientations that rise and subside, but always seem to rearise, because the hunger is always there, the need to revivify habituated, reflex-tending forms of life, and to do it collectively. We look forward to the connections between different approaches to participatory art-philosophy-political event design growing more dense and networked and expanded.

Joel McKim: One of the things that I think is interesting about the approach is that it is both concerned with the creative limitations required for producing an event and also concerned with how various events resonate with each other and amplify each other. This seems to bring us back to the problem we discussed earlier regarding how an affective politics may have a global presence, or work up to a scale larger than a single event.

Brian Massumi: Yes, a micropolitical event can have broad range. What qualifies it as micropolitical is the way it happens, not the dimensions it takes. By micropolitical we mean returning to the generative moment of experience, at the dawning of an event, to produce a modulatory commotion internal to the constitution of the event. It's a question of reconnecting processually with what's germinal in your living, with the conditions of emergence of the situations you live through. The idea is then to find a mechanism to pass that reconnection forward. Not impose it, not even suggest it as a general model. Rather, to give it as a gift, a gift of self-renewing process. This question of event-propagation, of processual seeding as part of a gift economy of revivifying experience, is the problem of a large-scale micropolitics. The process itself has to be self-valorizing. It has to have a value in itself because the situation of the world, Obama notwithstanding, is not overall one of hope. The situation of the world is desperate. There's no rational ground for hope. If you look at things rationally, if you look at the increasing disparities of wealth and health in the world, if you look at the spreading environmental destruction, if you look at the looming disasters in the foundations of the economy, if you look at the energy crisis and the food crises affecting the globe, and especially if you look at the way they interrelate, if you look at the virulence of renascent nationalist sentiment and of the culture of war, there is no hope. So the micropolitical question is how to live more intensely, live more fully, with augmented powers of existence, within the limits of that desperate situation, while finding ways to continue nevertheless, chipping away at the macro problems.

There's a certain incompleteness to any micropolitical event, like the SenseLab events I was talking about. A lot of things participants feel were on the verge of taking shape didn't quite happen. Potentials that you could just glimpse didn't come into focus. The goal is not to over-come the incompleteness. It's to make it compelling. Compelling enough that you are moved to do it again, differently, bringing out another set of potentials, some more formed and focused, others that were clearly expressed before now backgrounded. That creates a small, moveable environment of potential. The goal is to live in that moveable environment of potential. If you manage to, you will avoid the paralysis of hopelessness. Neither hope nor hopelessness – a pragmatics of poten-tial. You have to live it at every level. In the way you relate to your partner, and even your cat. The way you teach a class if you're a professor. The way you create and present your art if you're an artist. If you participate in more punctual events like the ones I was describing, this will provide a continuous background for what comes of those events to disseminate into and diffuse through. A symbiosis of the special event and the day-to-day, in creative connivance.

This is not to say that operating in a more macro, top-down, manner is wrong or should not be under-taken. It's just to say that if it's done to the exclusion of micropolitical activity it's mortifying, even when it's done for survival's sake. Sometimes there is no alterna-tive but to centrally impose certain enabling constraints. For example, I'd be very happy if the transition to a renewable-energy future or a global redistribution of wealth or a non-growth paradigm were imposed on the capitalist system. But high-level solutions of that kind are only part of the political equation, and it's not the part that the affective politics we've been talking about specifically addresses. Micropolitics is not programmatic. It doesn't construct and impose global solutions. But it would be naïve to think that it was separate from that kind of macro-activity. Anything that augments powers of existence creates conditions for micropolitical flourishings. No body flourishes without enough food and without health care. Micropolitical interventions need macro solutions. But success at the macropolitical level is at best partial without a complementary micropolitical flourishing. Without it, the tendency is towards standardization. Since macropolitical solutions are generally applicable by definition, by definition they act to curtail the variety and exuberance of forms of life. Macropolitical intervention targets minimal conditions of survival. Micropolitics complements that by fostering an excess of conditions of emergence. That inventiveness is where new solutions start to crystallize. The potentials produced at the micropolitical level feed up, climbing the slope that macropolitics descends. Micropolitical and macropolitical go together. One is never without the other. They are processual reciprocals. They aliment each other. At their best, they are mutually corrective. Even macro solutions designed to curtail micropolitical activity often end up feeding it by making it a necessity to invent new ways of getting by and getting around. Creative variation is the only real constant of politics. Deleuze and Guattari often made this point, for example in their slogan that the state is built on what escapes it.

It has become a commonplace recently to say that we are in a situation where the end of the world is now imaginable – but the end of capitalism isn't. That is definitely one 'solution' that is not likely to come pro- grammatically, top-down – given who's on top. The dismantling of capitalism is a 'corrective' that will only come from a breaking of the reciprocity I was just talking about between the macro- and micropolitical. The prevailing operating conditions of macro-/micro- political reciprocity should not be taken to imply that the symmetry is never broken, that a bifurcation can never occur. The complementarity can be broken in both directions. When macro-structures miniaturize themselves and work to usurp the ground of the micro- political with scaled-down versions of the dominant generalities, that is fascism. When micropolitical flour- ishings proliferate to produce a singularity, in the sense of a macrosystemic tipping point, that's revolution. The ultimate vocation of micropolitics is this: enacting the unimaginable. The symmetry-breaking, the point at which the unimaginable eventuates, is but a cut, 'smaller' than the smallest historically perceivable interval. That is to say, qualitatively different. A moment of a different colour, one you never see coming, that comes when it's least expected. Inevitably, a next micro/macro comple- mentarity will quickly settle in. But it will take a form that could not have been predicted, but is now suddenly doable and thinkable. Micropolitics is what makes the unimaginable practicable. It's the potential that makes possible.

3
Ideology and Escape

Yubraj Aryal*: Why do you think that 'affect' is more important for understanding how power operates in capitalism today, rather than concepts such as ideology and class? Are we living in a 'post-ideological' society, or a 'society after ideology'? What is the fate of ideology today?

Brian Massumi: To speak of a post-ideological society is to posit implicitly that society was effectively structured by ideology previously. This focuses the discussion on a negative claim: that a rupture has occurred. To support that claim, the received description of what one is claiming has been left must be taken as a starting point. The entire discussion remains framed in terms of the concept it is calling into question. Deleuze and Guattari do not

* Interview by Yubraj Aryal (2012)

refer to society after ideology. They make a much more radical claim: *'There is no ideology, and there never was.'* This is not the conclusion of their argument, but the beginning. What they are saying with this provocation is that the entire problem must be reframed, from start to finish. The conceptual strands that were bound together into the notion of ideology must be untied, and their connection to each other reproblematized. In the process, the presuppositions informing that construction must be re-examined.

In very broad strokes, the basic presuppositions informing the notion of ideology are that society is a structure, and that mechanisms of power defend and reproduce that structure. The structure is an organized whole composed of parts that have specifiable functions and occupy determinate positions within the whole. The relations among the parts have a coherence dictated by the structure of the whole they compose and whose general interests they serve. The coherence of the composition is a certain form of rationality, expressible as a set of mutually cohering propositions – in short, reflected in a structure of ideas. The task of the notion of ideology is to explain a thorny problem that then arises. Namely, that what is in the 'general interest' of the structure will never coincide with the specific interests of many of the subordinated working parts. It is likely, however, to coincide quite nicely with one of society's parts, or a small set of them, occupying a linchpin position. The 'general interest' is always really a 'dominant interest'. Now if the structure embodies a rationality expressible in a coherent structure of ideas, why is it that the subordinated parts – call them 'classes'

– accept their place? Why can't they see how the rationality coheres, and what it really means for them? Why don't they get the idea? Why can't they see through the mirage of the 'general' interest and understand it for what it is – a euphemism for the interests of a dominating class?

This is where affect enters the picture for ideological analysis. The structure of ideas must be inculcated without making it explicit. The reigning rationality must be transmitted, but occulted, hidden, distorted. To do this, it must pass through another medium: it must be translated onto an affective register. The dominated classes must be induced to mistake their own interests for the mirage of the 'general' interest – and do so with passion. They must be duped into affectively investing in the mechanisms of power that oppress them, without ever noticing the contradiction. They must become the willing instruments of their own domination. This is most efficiently done by weaving ways of feeling and acting that are in consonance with the power structure of society into the habitual fabric of everyday life, where they go on working unexamined. Ideology works best when its structure of ideas is lived – *acted out* in the everyday, without being thought out (as in Bourdieu's 'habitus').

The notion of ideology does not simply dismiss notions of affect. Rather, it mobilizes them in a particular way. Affect is seen as fundamentally delusional. But its illusions are useful. It provides the invitational opening for a rationality to get its hooks into the flesh. Affect is the domain of 'mere' feeling. It represents the vulnerability of the individual to larger societal forces.

Power hooks into the individual through feeling, and then pulls the strings that lead the individual into deluded acquiescence to its assigned role.

That society is a structure is just one of the presuppositions involved. There is a series of further presuppositions associated with it. There is the assumption that affect, or feeling, is individual. Also, that affect is the opposite of rational, that it is simply the irrational. It further assumes that if individuals were not affectively misled for ideological purposes, they would have the possibility of overcoming their own irrationality, in order to begin to act in accordance with their true interests. This contains the very traditional – and, one might add, thoroughly 'bourgeois' – assumption that self-interest is the primary motivating force, and that to act according to one's interests is to act rationally. It is precisely because this presupposition is lurking in the background that the critique of the dominant ideology must concern itself with the construction of the 'new man' (or whatever equivalent term is used). This is a collective project to make the general interest a reality. Individuals' ways of feeling and acting must recompose into a new rationality that abolishes the distance between individual and collective interest. Structure of feeling must be made to coincide with a new social coherence. Affect must be made to consciously coincide with the structure of ideas reflecting that coherence. The individual must come to affectively embody the collective structure, and live it in the everyday.

But how can this undoing of ideology be achieved – without inculcating a counter-ideology? How can a counter-ideology be inculcated without applying new mechanisms of power? How can those who most directly apply those mechanisms of power not become a new class, with its own special interests (the critical-ideological avant-garde turning into an apparatchik class)? How can those special interests not re-appeal to affect in an attempt to maintain the now resurgent mirage of the 'general' interest? In short, how can the dominant ideology be changed without imposing a new one that in the end reinscribes much the same structure, and works with much the same presuppositions, as the old one – and is no less a structure of domination?

It is as much for these practical reasons as for philosophical reasons that Deleuze and Guattari launch the rallying cry, 'there is no ideology and there never was'. Philosophically, the call is for a reframing of the problem in a way that strives to answer questions such as these:

1   Does it really make sense to think of society as a structure? Is it not more useful to think of it as a *process*? A process is dynamic and open-ended, composed of ongoing variations on itself. It fundamentally lacks the groundedness of a structure. Any stabilizing structuring is *emergent*, and self-improvised. This makes variation and change more fundamental than the reproduction of the same. The question is inverted. It is no longer: how is change possible, given the embeddedness of ideological reproduction in the social structure? Instead, the question is: how are certain regularities enabled to *re-emerge*, across the variations, in always new forms? A process is oriented, but as an evolving open whole. It is not self-consistent, and cannot be reduced to a structure of ideas and their functional

embodiments. It is, rather, a reciprocal implication of operations. It is not functional, but *operative*. It is not structured, but emergently *self-structuring*. Deleuze and Guattari need to clear away the old baggage of ideology critique in order to think capitalist society as a dynamic process of always ongoing self-structuration.

2 From this point of view, what ideology critique identifies as a determining foundation is a result: a product of process, a processual derivative. Process coagulates into re-emergent *regularities* which ideology critique tends to reify into *parts*, understood as societal building blocks such as classes. A dynamic process is not composed of parts. It is composed of operations that are directly *relational* in nature. By directly relational, I mean that the terms in relation do not pre-exist their relation and then enter into it. They are produced by the relation, and spin off from it. This is very much in keeping with the letter of Marx's thought. It is the *capitalist relation* that lies at the heart of his thinking. The worker and the capitalist do not simply enter into this relation. They are *constituted* by it. Their constitution itself is the regularity of certain spin-off effects that are contrived to accumulate – namely, effects of inequality, unequal access, unequal distribution. The accumulation coagulates in such a way as to determine the capitalist relation to return, ever more insistently, with ever more regularity, pushing ever further into new frontiers. It is less the capitalist structure of society that reproduces itself than the capitalist relation that self-proliferates, always expanding its field. 'Class' is a name for this processual accumulation of inequality operating within certain historical parameters of regularity. This changes the status of categories like 'worker' and 'capitalist'.

Marx does not just say that the capitalist identifies with the capitalist structure of society, and that the worker becomes affectively invested in it. He says that the capitalist *personifies* the capitalist relation's power to produce, and to appropriate productive forces ever more extensively, and ever more intensely. The worker personifies the potential for the capitalist relation to continue to appropriate productive forces as it proliferates and intensifies its operations – but also the potential that its operation hit a wall (of fatigue, of sabotage, of resistance). In other words, worker and capitalist are *figures* of capital. They index its constitutive tensions and tendencies. They are products of its process that figure the relational dynamic of its operations. These processual figures can then be fed back into the process to generate second-order effects (effects of processual self-reference).

Relation comes first, ontologically vis-à-vis persons, as well as politically vis-à-vis structure. Relation is primary. Since the capitalist relation proliferates in an open, complex, changing, fundamentally unpredictable field of ever-occurring events, its spin-off effects cannot be entirely stablized. The regularization is only ever provisional, the stability only ever a 'metastability', a provisional stability. Differences we identify as class differences (expressing the effects of unequal distribution) are continually produced by the capitalist process – emphasis on 'continually'. The capitalist process is continually in the process of refiguring itself, as it navigates the complexity of its stochastically challenged, open field of operation. What class means, what differences that notion figures, change fundamentally from one phase of capitalism to another, to the point of

Ideology and Escape

changing its very nature relative to the preceding frame of reference. A phase-shift of that kind is currently occurring, coinciding with the financialization of capital as analysed by such thinkers as Christian Marazzi.[1] Financialized capitalism's extreme complexity, precarity and pure operativity – so abstract an operativity as to be almost beyond all logic – spectacularly expressed themselves in the 2007–8 crisis. The financialization of capital complicates the scenario in fundamental ways. What does it mean to 'personify' a derivative? A credit default swap?

The call to go beyond ideology is a call to attend to the novelty of this situation, and to find ways of conceptualizing the current mode of operation of the capitalist process, and the new kinds of spin-off effects it produces, that are capable of grasping its novelty and complexity. How can a relational approach give us a new understanding of capitalism as a self-proliferating process? What are the new figures of that relation? Is the figuring still a question of personification? If so, is identification still at the basis of the figures of capital? If capitalism's operativity has become so complex, its 'instruments' so abstract, as to defy logic – and yet remain intensely effective – is it still a 'rationality'? If it is not a rationality, how can we continue to speak of ideology – the very construction of which posits a logos, an ideational foundation? What does all this mean for resistance?

3 The implication of Deleuze and Guattari's calling into question of ideology is that for the understanding

[1] Christian Marazzi, *The Violence of Financial Capitalism* (New York: Semiotext(e), 2010).

of capitalism as a process the concept of *affectivity* is more fundamental than rationality. A primacy of affect is a necessary corollary of the primacy of relation. But for the concept of affect to be useful here, it must be reconceptualized. It must be rethought in a way that understands it not as fundamentally individual, but as directly collective (as pertaining to relation). And it cannot be reduced to 'feeling' as opposed to thinking. It has to be understood as *involving feeling in thinking*, and vice versa. This requires revisiting the whole notion of rationality – and self-interest. In a process-oriented frame, the thinking-feeling of affect is always directly implicated in an operativity – *it pertains more fundamentally to events than to persons*. It is directly enactive. What is this enactive thinking-feeling, and what difference does it make in how we can think about capitalism as a mode of power, and about resistance?

Yubraj Aryal: What exactly is this new concept of affectivity, then? If it is a mode of thinking, how does it alter our concepts of rationality and thought – which, I presume, are not equivalent? And how can this affectivity function as a resistance to powers of domination and control?

Brian Massumi: The concept of affect that I find most useful is Spinoza's well-known definition. Very simply, he says that affect is 'the capacity to affect or be affected'. This is deceptively simple. First, it is directly relational, because it places affect in the space of relation: between an affecting and a being affected. It focuses on the middle, directly on what happens *between*. More than that, it forbids separating passivity from activity.

The definition considers 'to be affected' a *capacity*. The force of a blow, for example, is a product of an impinging force *meeting* a force of resistance, a certain capacity to resist. That capacity is a mode of activity of the body. It is a doing, as much as the blow itself (it is the body asserting its structural integrity, bracing itself in a certain manner to absorb, deflect, dodge the blow, or even, as in martial arts, to turn its force back against its author). Reciprocally, the fist that delivers the blow does not just affect its target. It is also affected by the force of resistance it encounters. To hit can hurt almost as much as to be hit. But the shared pain corresponds to a distribution of roles. The distribution of roles attaches the mode and degree of activity. The outcome may give one party a certain advantage in a next encounter. The relative standing of the parties involved may change in a way that has lasting effects. If those lasting effects stabilize into an inequality between the parties that conditions subsequent encounters, the structuring of an emergent power structure has occurred.

A blow is what it does. What it does is trigger the eventful resolution of a *differential* of forces at a point of *encounter*. The Spinozist definition hinges affect on encounter. It is thoroughly eventful, it derives structure from event. The two sides between which the encounter passes cannot simply be characterized as passive or active. The affective event does not presuppose a passivity on one side and an activity on the other. It involves a differential of modes and degrees of activity that is eventfully resolved, to structuring effect. This is very much in keeping with Michel Foucault's definition of power as a complex differential of forces, where the power to affect is strictly coincident with the power to resist, and where power effects accumulate. This places power structures and their corresponding roles on the level of effect, or of what comes to be eventfully determined. Power can no longer be construed as resting on an ideological ground that is predetermining. So the first step towards mobilizing a theory of affect for resistance is to understand that there is a first degree of resistance in any encounter that it is not simply passive, but already expresses a capacity, and that it is these encounters that are determining. There is no ideology as determining, in the first or last instance. Power structures are secondary effects of affective encounters, and ideologies are secondary expressions of power structures. Ideology is on the side of effects – twice over. It is not fundamentally on the side of causes. What it is certainly not is a sufficient cause.

The complexity of this model of affect quickly compounds. There is a second part to the definition. Affect, Spinoza says, is the capacity to affect or be affected, as applied to a *transition*. Further, the transition is *felt*, as the passing of a threshold to a higher or lower power of existence, understood as an affective readiness for subsequent encounter. That readiness carries resistance to the extent that it is unsubordinated to the roles unequally assigned by already-established power structures. It is with the notion of affect as involving a felt transition that we move, as you indicated in your question, away from the paradigm of rationality, while preserving *thought*. In the heat of an encounter, we are immersed in eventful working-out of affective capacities. We have no luxury of a distance from the event from which we can observe and reflect upon it. But in that immediacy of feeling absorbed in the encounter, we already understand, in the very fibre of our being, what is at stake, and where things might be tending. The feeling of the transitional encounter is not 'raw' feeling. It is imbued with an immediate understanding of what is under way, what might be coming – and what we are becoming. This is *enactive* understanding; it is one with the action. It is what I call a *thinking-feeling*. Thinking-feeling corresponds roughly to C.S. Peirce's category of 'abduction', which he considers the most primary of logical categories, lying at the root of the other, better-known logical modes, of induction and deduction.

It is clear that the affective thinking-feeling is not the thinking or feeling of a particular object – or a particular subject. It pertains more directly to the event, what passes in-between objects *and* subjects, than to the objects or subjects per se. It is important to emphasize that it is pre-subjective, in the sense that it is so integral to the event's unfolding that it can only retrospectively be 'owned', or owned up to, in memory and post facto reflection, as a content of an individualized experience. But it is even more important to realize that 'pre-subjective' in this usage means *transindividual*. Affective thinking-feeling is transindividual in two senses. First, in the sense just mentioned, namely that it pertains directly to what is passing *between* the individuals involved, which is reducible to neither taken separately. And second, in the sense that it coincides with a *becoming* of the involved individuals. As an event, it is already carrying each beyond itself, making it other than it is just now, and already more than what it was just then.

Looked at from this perspective, affect is a *differential attunement* between two bodies in a joint activity of becoming. What I mean by differential attunement is that the bodies in encounter are both completely absorbed in the felt transition, but they are differently absorbed, coming at it asymmetrically, from different angles, living a different complexion of affecting-being affected, transitioning through the encounter to different outcomes, perhaps structured into different roles. But all of these differences are actively, dynamically co-implicated in the event, as immediate dimensions of the event, the *same* unfolding event. It is the same event that is integrally lived by both – integrally but heterogeneously; synchronously but asymmetrically. The event is the integral of the differences. It is the curve of their affective integration. The arc of their thought-felt, unfolding co-implication.

But why limit the discussion to two bodies? Life is full of situations including a plurality of bodies, similarly differentially attuned to an event playing through the situation. If you think of *media events* in particular, they involve multitudes of bodies. The example of the blow is just a convenient limit-case. Multiplicity is more the rule. For the concept of affect to take on its full force and furthest implications, it is necessary to think of it as involving a multiplicity. Every encounter between two bodies always has the potential to open up to more. The concept of affect applies most properly to *populations.*

Now if there is a complex transindividual thinking-feeling in a simple encounter between two bodies, how much more intensely is the transindividuality thought-felt in multi-body situations? If a simple encounter between two bodies like a blow involves resistance, and as such can be modulated as it occurs, the way martial arts modulate the affective force of a combat encounter, that means that there are *affect modulation techniques* accessible in the event. They become accessible to the event through reflex, habit, training and the inculcation of skills – automaticities operating with as much dynamic immediacy as the event, directly as part of the event. These automaticities cannot be reduced to slavish repetition, a lack of freedom to manoeuvre. In fact, as any musician will tell you, they are the necessary foundation for *improvisation*. You can only effectively improvise on the basis of elaborate forms of enactive knowing that operate with all the automaticity of a 'second nature'. What I am suggesting is that affect can be modulated by improvisational techniques that are thought-felt into action, flush with the event. This thinking-feeling of affect, in all its immediacy, can be *strategic*. Since it modulates an unfolding event on the fly, it cannot completely control the outcome. But it can inflect it, tweak it. So it is not strategic in the sense of preconceiving a specific outcome in all its detail and finding the means to arrive at that intended end. It is *all means* – all in the middle, in the midst, in the heat of encounter. It is directly participatory, at no distance from the event under modulation. It is the tweaking of an arc of unfolding, on the fly. It is therefore more akin to the deflection or inflection of an already active *tendency* than the imposition of a prescribed intention, or pre-intended prescription. But the inflection of tendency can also accumulate from one encounter to the next, and lead somewhere new. It can amplify, resonate or even bifurcate – potentially in ways that don't coagulate into a power structure, but instead keep restructuring, keep the structur*ing* alive. This is not a 'rationality'.

It's an *affectivity*, redolent with thought, flush with action.

Politically, this changes the whole framework. Affective techniques of thinking-feeling improvisationally are *relational techniques* that apply to situations more directly than to persons. They are directly collective. They are fundamentally participatory, since they are activated in situation, couched singularly in the occurrence of that encounter. They are event-factors, not intentions. My proposition is that there are relational techniques that can be practised to modulate unfolding events in a way that takes off from the primary capacity of resistance implied in a Spinozist concept of affect, and have the potential of reorienting tendencies towards different ends, without predesignating exactly what they are. This avoids the ideological trap of ending up reimposing much the same kind of power structure that is being resisted. Tendencies are oriented, but open-ended. An in-situation, on-the-fly modulation can be complexly co-inflected by any number of bodies, so that the integral of the differences in play that is what all those involved become in differential attunement to the same event will always be an irreducibly collective product. It is a collective self-structuring. This is a politics beyond self-interest, but not in any 'general' interest. It is in the interests of the collectively unfolding *event*.

For me, this is the foundation for practices of direct democracy, lived democracy, democracy as essentially participatory and irreducibly relational, practised as an improvisational *event mechanics* (to borrow the title of Glen Fuller's philosophical blog). This is a democracy whose base concept is not the supposed freedom of the individual from the collectivity, but the freedom *of* the

(off)

collectivity, *for* its becoming. It is the embodied freedom of bodies to come together in thinking-feeling, to participate in differentially attuned becoming, in all immediacy and with all urgency.

The activities that Erin Manning and I co-organize through her philosophical laboratory, the SenseLab, attempt to experiment with improvisational techniques of relation from this transindividual perspective of event mechanics. Movement-events like the Arab Spring, Occupy, the Spanish *indignados* movements, and the 2012 student movement we in Quebec call the Maple Spring can be seen as collective embodiments of this kind of democracy in action.[2] Anywhere representation is eschewed in favour of presentation, in the sense of affective tuning-in; anywhere the square or the street takes precedence over the party meeting; anywhere directly embodied participation takes the upper hand from the communication of opinion or the prescription of intended outcomes; anywhere decision is an emergent property of the coming-together, for becoming-together, of a differential human multiplicity, and not the edict of an individual leader or lead group backed by an existing power structure of whatever stripe – there, a direct democracy is being improvised. There, resistance is unfolding.

Yubraj Aryal: Your earlier appeal to a 'process-oriented frame' brings to mind Whitehead, who is not generally

[2] *Quebec's Maple Spring*, special supplement to *Theory & Event*, ed. Darin Barney, Brian Massumi, and Cayley Sochoran, vol. 15, no. 3 (September 2012), http://muse.jhu.edu/journals/theory_and_event/toc/tae.15.3S.html

Resistance

considered to be a political thinker. Do I sense in your response a conviction that Whitehead's metaphysics can be a useful resource in thinking through these issues?

Brian Massumi: Yes, very much so. But I also understand how Whitehead's own vocabulary, when it comes to social and political issues, can make one cringe. From our historical vantage point, and in particular from a non-Eurocentric perspective, it is difficult to abide such terms as 'progress' and 'civilization' as the basis for political thinking. But if you look at what Whitehead was getting at through those now tainted terms, his thinking remains highly relevant today. When he speaks of 'civilization' it is not with reference to any form of group identity. Instead, he speaks of contrast. Basically, what he calls the civilizing process is the ability to hold contrasts together. It's about making forms or formations that have tended to mutually exclude each other cohabit the same field, not in spite of their difference, but affirming it as a value. This involves relational techniques for creating inclusive field conditions making what was mutually exclusive *compossible*. The mutual inclusion of contrasting forms in the same field is an *intensification* of that field. 'Progress' for Whitehead is the achievement of ever greater intensity. It is not a linear advance towards a predesignated end. It is not teleological. It is the *invention* of new fields of mutual inclusion, and that invention has all the singularity of the collectively self-structuring events I was just talking about, which have tendency but without teleology.

Intensity does not 'have' value. Intensity *is* a value, in itself. In fact, it is a surplus-value: a *surplus-value of life*. It is a more to life, in life, one with its improvisational thinking-feeling. This way of thinking about politics in terms of contrasts and lived intensities of feeling is unmistakeably aesthetic in tenor. Whitehead was one of the first philosophers to create an *aesthetico-politics*. I find many resonances between his aesthetico-political approach and Félix Guattari's 'ethico-aesthetic paradigm', in which I find much inspiration.[3] The concept of the integral mutual inclusion of contrasts in a shared dynamic field is close to the notion of 'differential attunement' I was using earlier. Whitehead's proposition to make a fundamental value of the mutual inclusion of differences makes the invaluable point that the goal of politics need not be the overcoming of differences, or even their reconciling. Instead, the goal can be their rendering compossible, *as* different, with all the intensity that can be had in their eventful in-between.

Yubraj Aryal: For Deleuze, a crucial political question is: how can we free ourselves from the condition under which we tend to 'fight for our servitude as stubbornly as though it were our salvation'? Can the performative quality of affective political resistance help prevent us from investing in a social system that constantly represses us, thwarts our interests, and introduces lack into our lives? Can a faith in 'affect' help ensure our freedom within or from such powers of domination and control?

Brian Massumi: Affect, for me, is not a matter of faith. I would worry about any interpretation of the concept

[3] Félix Guattari, *Chaosmosis: An Ethico-Aesthetic Paradigm*, trans. Paul Bains and Julian Pefanis (Bloomington: Indiana University Press, 1995).

in those terms. Faith in affect would be as misguided as faith in supposedly disinterested reason. For me, the question is two-fold. On the one hand, it is purely pragmatic; on the other, it is in a certain way aesthetic. Pragmatically, the question concerns powers of existence – powers to act, think and feel. Can strategies privileging an affective approach to events increase our powers of existence? Can they help us act differently, think more actively and feel more thinkingly? If the answer is yes – and I think it is – then they are intensifiers of existence, and produce what I just called a surplus-value of life. A surplus-value of life is a surplus-value of experience: an enactively lived and immediately felt qualitative difference expressing a heightening of capacities. It is a felt excess of potential, over and above any particular state of being. That could stand quite well as a definition of aesthetic value. Affective approaches embody a pragmatist aesthetics of life's living.

The question of servitude is actually complicated by this perspective. There is nothing essentially liberatory or progressive about affect. Deleuze and Guattari were haunted by the problem of what they called 'microfascism'. That is the idea that oppressive structures (like the state) can only bear down from above because they have first risen up from below. They are crystallizations of tendencies that have amplified and settled into a self-reproducing structure. Power structures are structurations *of* affective tendencies. They are emergent, and like all emergences, their seat is the seat of affect – what I call 'bare activity', or the activated thinking-feeling body in its radical openness to events and to other bodies, in affective attunement. Structures of oppression not only have their seat in bare activity, they must continually return to it, fold themselves back into it, to come back out through it. This is because, as I said earlier about 'society', higher-order structurations are emergent. As they emerge, they settle into 'apparatuses of capture'. By 'settled' I mean that they contrive to re-emerge. As they do so, they capture affective tendencies originating in the open field of embodied collective attunement, and feed off of them, feed them into their own perpetuation. Structures of oppression are regularities of capture. Prior to capture, in their first stirrings in the existential field of bare activity, the movements a structure feeds off of belong to a different order from the one they are structured into. They belong to an order of incipiency of a very different texture. Structures of power are powered by these different-order movements that they capture. They are parasitic. Vampiric. They emerge, self-structuring, surfing the crest of outside energies, and can only perpetuate themselves by diving in and catching the wave again. They have no motive force of their own.

The idea that structures of power are powered by energies originating outside their order is encapsulated by Deleuze and Guattari in the paradoxical political formula that *structures are 'defined by what escapes them'*. They are always running after different-order movements in the collective field of embodied activity in order to funnel them back into their own channels. A 'rationality' is nothing more than the logic of a channelling of that kind. All rationalizations have their seat in affect, and remain creatures of affect – all high-minded protestations to the contrary.

All of this complicates the question of servitude because it means that there is no pure realm free of power. If structures of power are always running after different-order movements to feed on, it means that they find ways to feed their own alimentary operations back into the field of emergence. They contaminate the field. They convert movements afoot in the field to their own ends. Among them are tendencies already moving in ways that lend themselves to capture – formative forces of emergence that come in a way conversion-ready. These 'microfascist' tendencies are Nietzsche's 'reactive forces', which he analysed in *The Genealogy of Morals* under the concept of 'ressentiment'. Reactive forces, in Deleuze's words, are those which 'separate other forces from what they can do'. They are tendencies towards repetition (reduction of difference), stabilization and rest (de-intensification), division and subsumption (divide and conquer). Deleuze develops a fascinating account of the relation between active and reactive forces in his book on Nietzsche.[4] One of my earliest books, *First and Last Emperors: The Absolute State and the Body of the Despot*,[5] explored the constitutive tensions of the reactive forces as they amplify in scale and play out society-wide. For the present discussion, the important point in the notion of microfascism is that there is no original state of freedom that is somehow fettered, but to which we can nurse the dream to return. The seeds of oppression are always already sown, and are always already in play. Affective dynamics not only

[4] Gilles Deleuze, *Nietzsche and Philosophy*, trans. Hugh Tomlinson (New York: Columbia University Press, 1983).
[5] Kenneth Dean and Brian Massumi, *First and Last Emperors: The Absolute State and the Body of the Despot* (New York: Autonomedia, 1992).

can but are destined to give rise to oppressive structures. Servitude, as much of oneself as of others, servitude to structures of power at whatever level, is energetically, collectively *desired*. In the 1930s the 'masses', Deleuze and Guattari say, were not ideologically duped into submitting to fascism. They positively desired it. They actively affirmed it. Fascism emerged from the bare-active stirrings of a mode of collective affective attunement tending towards ressentiment, which it amplified and reinforced, organized and returned to, then fed off in an infernal cycle.

Yubraj Aryal: Then 'what can a body do'? How can it resist power? In other words, how can we mobilize our body in order to constitute what Foucault called 'techniques of the self' (to practise our freedom and create a 'style of existence') within or beyond the 'techniques of domination' of power in capitalism?

Brian Massumi: It goes both ways. Although there is no original state of freedom to which we can return, if structures of power are defined by what escapes them, then resistance is as much a part of the collective field as the tendency for capture by techniques of domination. This was Foucault's basic point: power and resistance are two sides of the same coin. Tendencies towards free action, towards escape from crystallized power structures, are as primary as the tendency towards capture I was just talking about. A power*ed* structure is not all-encompassing. It rises from a field of emergence that includes *it*. It is plugged into a broader field of activity on which it feeds. That field is astir with tendencies pointing to the potential for different modes

of structuration. They may not amplify past the point of incipiency, they may be captured, or simply fail to take and subside back into the field of bare activity from which they came, but still their difference cannot not have been felt at some level, in some way. So even if there is no unsullied *state* of freedom to return to, there is always a *degree* of freedom offering the potential for other emergences. There are always counter-tendencies that can be joined, and moved with, proposing themselves for amplification. There is always a margin of manoeuvre. What a body can do is tweak the field – improvise modulations of the field of activity in a way that takes up the offer of these different-order affective tendencies. What a body can do is trigger counter-amplifications and counter-crystallizations that defy capture by existing structures, streaming them into a continuing collective movement of escape. If the movement effects an intensification of the collective field through the mutual inclusion in it of reciprocally heightened capacities in contrastive attunement, then the degree of freedom has been increased across the board. Powers of existence have been collectively augmented. This can only occur from within, in situation, flush with the event, in an immediacy of enaction.

In this enactive immediacy, resistance is of the nature of a *gesture*. Resistance cannot be communicated or inculcated. It can only be gestured. The gesture is a call to attunement. It is an invitation to mutual inclusion in a collective movement. The only power it has is *exemplary*. It cannot impose itself. It can only catch on. Its power is to throw out the lure of its own amplification. Its power is of contagion. The gesture of resistance is a micro-gesture of offered contagion, oriented otherwise

Resistance is immanent critique

than towards the structures into which the gestures of microfascism occurring on the same level, in the same field, have the tendency to channel. All of this is very consistent with Gabriel Tarde's micro-sociology of 'imitation'. But it also reinforces the notion that there is an aesthetic dimension – of allure, of style of gesture – that is not an added dimension but is absolutely integral to the very operation of resistance, one with its politicality.

There is only one a priori: participation, participatory immersion in bare activity. Resistance comes of immanence. It cannot be led. If it is, it is already coagulating into an apparatus of capture poised to rise up and bear down, as if from above and outside. Resistance is *immanent critique*: a 'critique' that is one with its enaction. It occurs at the level on which bodies think more actively and feel more thinkingly, towards acting differently together. In this kind of resistance, there is no avant-garde. There are seeds. Seeds of free action blowing in the winds of bare activity, looking for a fertile field of attunement for their flowering. The analogy is inexact. Such a field does not exist. In its role as exemplary gesture, resistance creates its own field. It gestures it into existence, by its own power of contagion. Resistance is performative of itself. It triggers its own self-organizing. Its field is always to come, flush with its own self-amplifying event.

Immanent critique, as its name implies, cannot purport to apply already-established criteria of correctness or necessity to the field of collective action. It cannot operate in the imperative, based on a prior political programme or already structured set of moral precepts. It cannot *justify* itself by appealing to established

We don't really want to be free. JB

principles. It immanently enacts its own principle, which is one with its exemplary movement. There is no *ought* to resistance. On what basis can we say that it is better to desire one's freedom than one's servitude? That one 'ought' to resist? An 'ought' is nothing but an already assumed servitude to a higher order of imperative. To say 'ought' is to enact our servitude to abstract principle, and to justify our imposing it on others, as from outside and above. It's a power move. As such, it carries seeds of domination – perhaps a new order of domination, but domination nonetheless. Freedom, like oppression, is *desired*, or it is nothing at all. It cannot be 'oughted' and imposed. It cannot be inculcated. It is desired, or it is nothing. Resistance is the counter-desire for the collective augmentation of powers of existence, in dynamic mutual inclusion in an intensive field of contrasts. There is no basis on which we can say it is 'better' *in principle*. But there are ways to *perform* its desirability – to make it more desired, more strongly tended towards, more amplificatory and exemplary. There are indeed techniques of resistance. They are *techniques of relation* aimed at immanent field-modulation. They are gestures already in relation, in participatory immersion, stirring towards self-augmenting *relational movement*.

Deleuze + Guattari ??

on affect

Yes!

This is closer to the anarchist notion of 'propaganda by the deed' than it is to traditional Marxist notions of ideology critique and vanguard action. Over the last two years, we have seen this kind of exemplary politics percolating up in many places around the world. The Occupy movement's refusal to advance a particular set of demands is a case in point. This refusal to set forth a programme was not a deficiency, it was an enablement. It was a way of saying that what was important was the gathering together of bodies and capacities in self-improvising collective movement for the production of surplus-value of life, and that democracy *is* that far-from-equilibrium movement – not its pre-programmed end in a prefigured stable structure. This is the 'direct', relational democracy of enactive resistance.

There is a certain slippage that has occurred in our discussion. We began by discussing capitalism, and have ended up talking about structures of domination that are tacitly on the model of the state. Everything I have just said about microfascism and structures of domination has to be thoroughly reconceptualized in relation to capitalism. This is because capitalism, as I was saying at the beginning of this interview, is not a structure in any usual sense of the term. It is much too protean and fluidly self-organizing to be a structure. It is often called a 'system'. But even this is perhaps too static a concept. Capitalism is an open system, coextensive with society. It is so dynamically self-modulating that it is best to call it a 'process', in contradistinction both to 'structure' and to 'system'. It is self-modulating and self-amplifying, from a posture immanent to the field of life. It has fed its operations back into the field of emergence of bare activity so integrally as to become-immanent to it. The capitalist relation is everywhere, potentially. Every move made anywhere, from the farthest corner of the earth to the most intimate depths of the soul, is susceptible to capitalist capture.

This idea of capitalism's immanence to the field of life is what the concept of 'biopower' is often used to analyse, in the work of such thinkers as Maurizio

Lazzarato. The concept of biopower raises special issues that must be grappled with if we are to think usefully about capitalism as a form of power. Capitalism in its current phase as a self-modulating, self-amplifying process that is immanent to the field of life is always *escaping itself.* It is continually leading itself into *crisis,* from which it always finds ways to re-emerge, as a further variation on itself. In this self-reinventive movement of escape, capitalism *shares many of the characteristics of resistance.* In its own destructive way, it works affectively to foster emergent tendencies, improvise amplifications – and in so doing, intensify powers of existence. But it does so in a way that is always and everywhere answerable to the capitalist relation, and the distinction it implants between money as means of payment and money as capital (in Marx's shorthand, C-M-C' versus M-C-M'). Access to money as capital is by nature unequal, and the inequality has an inexorable tendency to increase. Capitalism augments powers of existence, but does so essentially unequally. It may produce a surplus-value of life, but it is unequally distributed because it is always in the service of surplus-value in the monetary-capital sense, with all the inequalities that come with it, and all the brutalities that come with that inequality. In a word, capitalism *captures resistance* towards its own unequal processual ends.

Capitalism's mantra is 'productivity'. In the era of biopower, what bodies are meant to produce is essentially their own economically productive lives – integrally self-converting into 'human capital'. Life itself has become integrally capital-intensive. Those away from whom the augmentation of powers of existence flows, those around whom the inequalities of the process accumulate, are not in a position to constitute them-selves as human capital to a 'competitive' degree. They are not in a position to personify the self-productive powers of the process of capital at full intensity. They are bemoaned as insufficiently 'productive'. They are left behind by the movement of capital. In a regime of biopower, they are as good as dead. The flipside of biopower is the 'necropolitics' theorized by Achille Mbembe in response to the debate on biopower.[6]

I call a process that augments powers of existence an *ontopower*. Capitalism has made itself a species of ontopower. The task of resistance in the contemporary age is not just to fight power, it is to learn how to fight this ontopower. The battle that is being waged on resist-ance's own home ground: ontopower against onto-power, on the same field of battle, flush with the same events, in immanent critique. There is no alternative to immanent critique. Capitalism is now effectively global. There is no outside of the capitalist process. There is no position from which to critique it from outside. It is in our bodies, in our lives' arising, in bare activity, in every little niche of the collective field.

Note!

The implications of capitalism's ontopowerful capture of resistance are far-reaching, and far from being clear. It is beyond the limits of this interview to explore them further. I have tried to work out some of the impli-cations in some of my recent work, in particular *The Power at the End of the Economy*[7] and *Ontopower*. I

OK

[6] Achille Mbembe, 'Necropolitics', *Public Culture*, vol. 15, no. 1 (winter 2003), pp. 11–40.
[7] Brian Massumi, *The Power at the End of the Economy* (Durham, NC: Duke University Press, 2015).

think new distinctions are necessary, not only among structure, system and process, but also between bio-power and ontopower (which for me actually goes even beyond biopower in its becoming-immanent to the field of life – a point of disagreement with Lazzarato), and concerning the relation of state (and state-like) structures to capitalism (for the state is one of the last refuges of supposedly rationalized structure – capitalism hardly bothers to assert its rationality any more, contenting itself with creating the affective 'fact' of its inevitability).

In any case, it's an ongoing project. We are in the midst – as always – and things will only begin to become clear as we continue to experiment collectively and participatorily, on the conceptual level in our writing and thinking, and afield experimentally, in thinking-feeling gestures of invitation to collective movement, on the street and in the institutions framing our daily activities. Like the field of resistance, the clarification is to come, flush with our exemplary events. To be invented...If faith in affect is misplaced, as Deleuze often said, 'belief in the world' is not. It's all we have: the participatory trust that the world always already offers degrees of freedom ready for amplification.

4

Affective attunement in the field of catastrophe

With Erin Manning

Bodil Marie Stavning Thomsen*: Brian, we were reading your article in *The Guardian* about the Fukushima nuclear power plant disaster, affective politics and the media.[1] Catastrophe used to be talked about as the exceptional. But nowadays, we see, it's ubiquitous. In your article you discuss the affective power of new media in relation to globalization and the risk

---

* Interview by Jonas Fritsch and Bodil Marie Stavning Thomsen (2011)

[1] Brian Massumi, 'The Half-Life of Disaster', *Guardian*, 15 April 2011, http://www.guardian.co.uk/commentisfree/2011/apr/15/half-life-of-disaster

---

society, relating it to catastrophes like Fukushima that reverberate everywhere, across all boundaries. In particular, the boundary between cultural production and natural forces is blurred today, it almost no longer applies, and our ability to act and how we are able to touch each other has been affected by the affective atmosphere of natural-cultural catastrophes, to the point where we have almost lost that ability. This sentence of the article caught our attention: 'An ecological alter-politics must also be an alter-politics of affect.'

Brian Massumi: Which I didn't explain at all.

Bodil Marie Stavning Thomsen: That was why we thought of bringing it up, thinking that maybe the concept of the 'biogram' that you develop in *Parables for the Virtual*[2] might be a way of re-figuring how we could actually react to or act towards those affective powers.

Brian Massumi: Well, I think that the kinds of contact we were used to having and that we experience as live and interpersonal have become dispersed. I don't think they've been replaced by a disconnect, but by a different kind of contact that is just as affectively charged. And yes, it's clear that crisis and catastrophe are no longer exceptional, they're the normal situation, as Benjamin famously said. The complexity of the interlocking systems we live in, on the social, cultural, economic and

[2] Brian Massumi, *Parables for the Virtual: Movement, Affect, Sensation* (Durham, NC: Duke University Press, 2002), pp. 177–207.

natural levels, is now felt in all its complexity, because we're reaching certain tipping points, for example in relation to climate change and refugee flows. There is a sense that we're in a far-from-equilibrium situation where each of the systems we have depended upon for stability is perpetually on the verge of tipping over into crisis, with the danger that there will be a sort of cascade of effects through adjoining systems, like a domino effect. It's a very unstable, quasi-chaotic situation. And there's no vantage point from which to understand it from the outside. We're immersed in it. We're absorbed in the imminence of catastrophe, always braced for it – which means it has become imm*a*nent to our field of life. That imminence-immanence is a mode of contact, of direct affective proximity, even if it occurs 'at a distance' through the action of the media or, more to the point, within an increasingly integrated media ecology.

When we talk about how affect works now, I think we have to start from the fact that we are all braced in that field of immi(a)nence. Our bodies and our lives are almost a kind of resonating chamber for media-borne perturbations that strike us and run through us, that strike us and strike beyond us simultaneously. This is all happening at a level· before we can position ourselves, before we are able to step back and try to rationalize the experience. We are braced into the experience, inducted into it in a very direct, bodily way, before we can adopt a considered posture towards it. That's why I talk about 'immediation' in *Semblance and Event*.[3]

---

[3] Brian Massumi, *Semblance and Event: Activist Philosophy and the Occurrent Arts* (Cambridge, MA: MIT Press, 2011).

I use the model of the event to talk about what has been traditionally analysed in terms of mediation and transmission. What I'm talking about is more an immediate in-bracing than a mediation in the traditional sense. This in-bracing has more to do with complex field effects, and their wave-like amplification and propagation, than with point-to-point transmissions.

From this perspective, the question is then what happens in the field, in all immediacy? It seems to me that rather than personally positioning each individual, it braces them into a kind of differential attunement with others. We're all in on the event together, but we're in it together differently. We each come with a different set of tendencies, habits and action potentials. That's what I mean by differential attunement: a collective in-bracing in the immediacy of an affective event, but differently in each case. 'Attunement' refers to the direct capture of attention and energies by the event. 'Differential' refers to the fact that we each are taken into the event from a different angle, and move out of it following our own singular trajectories, riding the waves in our own inimitable way. It's the idea of an event snapping us to attention together, and correlating our diversity to the affective charge this brings, energizing the whole situation. And it's the idea that this happens at a level where direct bodily reactions and our ability to think are so directly bound up with each other that they can't be separated out yet from each other, or from the energizing of the event.

I don't believe that our condition is homogenizing, as so many critiques of the contemporary media environment say, or that things work in the first instance by positioning the individual, as ideological critique might say – even though there are certain presuppositions that get performatively implanted in the field, and certain tendencies already vectorizing it, in a kind of proto-organization of what is happening. The main point is it's all happening far-from-equilibrium, so that what counts is the fielding of instability, and the fact that unpredictable order-out-of-chaos effects can always disable, deviate or reconfigure any pre-organization. So when I'm talking about affect I'm talking about a directly relational immersion in a field of immi(a)nence from which determined actions and determinate thoughts have to emerge. They have to be extracted from the field of complexity on the fly, performatively.

The question then becomes, what modulates the extraction? Overall it's modulated by the feeling of threat that comes with the sense of emergency, and by the securitization procedures that have been set in place in response. But securitization assumes instability. Security is not the opposite of insecurity. It's wed to it. In his book on trust and power, Niklas Luhmann is clear about that.[4] To produce security with any regularity, he says, you have to produce the insecurity it's predicated on. Foucault makes the same point. Security measures have to be taken pre-emptively, because we're always caught in the first flush of something happening under complex emergency conditions, before it can be known where it will go and what it will become. Security measures have to bootstrap order back out of quasi-chaos. I've argued that this qualifies them as procedures of becoming, or what I call 'ontopower'.

[4] Niklas Luhmann, *Trust and Power* (New York: John Wiley & Sons, 1979).

So the question of affective politics for me is accepting that we're in that field of collective differential attunement that triggers a collective individuation, and that we're always being thrown back into it in a direct, immersive, immediated way, and then asking what counter-ontopower we can exercise to get ourselves out of that securitization loop. How can we exert some influence flush with that immersion, but disabling or disenabling the presuppositions of securitization? How can we implant new presuppositions, and proto-organize more liveable and convivial tendencies? How can we implant new tendencies into that hyper-complex ecological field of life? I think a concept like the biogram is a very good place to begin. The biogram is a version of Gilles Deleuze's concept of the 'diagram', but applied to an individual life modulating its own course under conditions of complexity. To diagram, or biogram, is not to pre-define. It's a cartography of potential. It's about techniques for moving into and out of the immersive field of life complexity in a way that is oriented, or reorienting, but not in pre-articulated directions – inventively. Then the question is how you prolong the differential attunement, instead of coming out of it into your own personal trajectory. How do you capture the intensity of the in-bracing to remain corre-lated, to coordinate, to move inventively together in concerted action – crucially, without erasing the attuned differences?

Erin Manning: Also wouldn't you say that these fields of resonance are themselves creating biograms? So it's not about you bringing a biogram to the event but that the event is proliferating in a field that is itself biogrammatic? The question seems to me to be one of double capture in the way that Stengers defines it. So some of the biogrammatic tendencies will themselves be conductors for more resonance and some will fall by the wayside or will act in ways that are less foregrounded?

Brian Massumi: Exactly. A biogram is at the same time found and constructed. Putting those two together is not a contradiction – it's a process. The biogram is given by the circumstances, for its potential transformation. It is a live mapping of the process under transition – a kind of process gear-shift mechanism.

Bodil Marie Stavning Thomsen: In *Semblance and Event* you give the example of the Deleuzian time-image. You can't see the time-image. It's not explicitly there, but it's real, and could be aligned to a diagrammatic or biogrammatic thinking. In order to experience the time-image, you have to hold open the future – and the past that will have led to it. This is done by inserting virtual images into the interstice between the past and the future.

Brian Massumi: And you're in some way perceiving those virtualities without their *actually* presenting themselves to your senses.

Erin Manning: It's really a question of time, of different qualities of speeds and slownesses, but also of the undoing of the linear. Brian, your rendering of affective politics happens in a verb tense that is itself looping. Pre-emption happens in a future anterior, in the will-have-been – but even the future anterior doesn't quite cover its capacity to proliferate.

Brian Massumi: Yes, there is a nonlinear temporality to it. I refer to Deleuze's time-image in *Semblance and Event*, but it's not exactly the same concerns that I'm trying to explore in that book. I use the term 'semblance' to develop the idea that there are dimensions of an event that are not actually present but are necessary factors for its constitution.

Take something as simple as a line of movement. It makes no sense to take it as a sequence of points, because that abstracts the movement out of it. As Bergson said, all you get is a set of points, and points are fixed. The movement is not a sequence of points. It's a folding of the immediate past into the present, as the present is turning over into the future, in a way that qualitatively changes a situation. The past and the future are necessary factors in the constitution of a trajectory of movement. But they are not actual, they're alreadys and not yets. So when something is in movement, it's exceeding itself dynamically, it is overspilling its actuality. It is more-than-present at each successive point. We understand that intuitively, we perceive it directly, without having to think about it. If you think of a political situation and the kind of collective differential attunement I was talking about – for example a disaster hitting that you have no way of knowing the exact nature or extent of yet – there's a large number of potential trajectories in play. The onset of the event crystallizes a field of potential movement. Think of it as a pragmatic field, made up of co-present vectors or potential trajectories that are immediately felt, intuitively understood, in an intensely embodied way, that call everyone to attention and energize us towards action – but are not yet actualized, that are more-than-present in their potential. That felt potential is the jumping-off point, it's in the very first flush of what's coming, so it can be treated as a presupposition of the event's unfolding. The potential is pragmatically presupposed.

So a way of thinking about this politically is in terms of pragmatic presuppositions that are perceptually felt without being thought out, but that retrospectively you could separate out as if they were the result of a judgement or a deduction or an inference. But this activation of presupposed potentials happens so quickly that no such judgement could have been made. It's completely on the level of immediate perception, even though it's non-actualized. You're non-sensuously feeling it. It's a kind of thinking-feeling of what's happening, including what *may* happen. The thing is, our thinking-feeling of what may happen includes what other people may do, in correlated but differential response, each following their particular tendencies. In a situation of disaster, the collective rush to safety may block a trajectory. Or someone may be already spontaneously offering a helping hand, setting an example to others that works like a kind of unplanned propaganda of the deed. At the very onset of an event, there are any number of these tendencies and condition-setting deeds coming together to create and modulate the unfolding of a very complex vectorial field that is directly collective – transindividual.

That's what we're experiencing today, that's what we're living, that's what we're thinking-feeling moment by moment in this atmosphere of crisis and impending catastrophe. So one of the questions of the biogram is how the pragmatic field of potential crystallizes for each person, given the kinds of events we are living through together, how the different attunements occur across individual differences. Then the next question is: are there ways of tweaking these kinds of pragmatic pre-suppositions, crystallizing a field that creates a greater availability of certain alternative tendencies, more of the helping-hand variety? That would be a modulation of the biogram. Can this alter collective conditions in a lasting way? Can the modulations be gathered up, archived, reactivated? Can techniques be found to make them more creative? These are the kinds of problems we've been working with in the SenseLab events, with an emphasis on this notion that there are creative techniques for the modulation of relational fields, and that it can help to think about them in diagrammatic, or biogrammatic, terms.

Jonas Fritsch: I'd like to talk about the dynamics of this particular field of relations. It feels as though it is both over-structured in a way – that you're caught in a kind of web – but also at the same time that it's over-open, in the sense that there are always different ways out. That kind of dynamic, I think, is best captured by distinguishing between attunement and the concepts, for instance, of transmission that you were talking about before. That idea of the transmission of affect is something that runs through the whole discourse on affect today. What is the difference between notions of the transmission or contagion of affect and the notion of attunement?

Erin Manning: You mean in the political sphere in particular?

Jonas Fritsch: I was thinking about the dynamics of the relational field and what working on an affective level entails. Because there is determination in a way but also this openness of potential.

Erin Manning: In my own work I have been thinking a lot about the tendency we have to play out the affective more than anything else in regard to the human. We've seen this a lot around the work of the so-called 'affective turn' where the human remains the bearer and conduit of affect. So I've been interested in exploring, in my own work but also with Brian and in the events we organize together, what I call the various 'speciations' that ecologies of affect produce. These ecologies are constituted biogrammatically or diagrammatically in the sense that they are tweakings of emergent tendencies for coalescence within a co-emergent field of experience. They are neither human nor nonhuman – more like resonance machines that are activated in the between of the organic and the inorganic. I think of speciations – the elbow-table-lean of this conversation, for instance – as a kind of coming-into-emergence of a welling individuation that connects as a remarkable point or a point of inflection to a wider field of experience – the summer, the house, the post-SenseLab-event conversation we are having. The singular 'speciation' of this current time-signature activates the wider field of relation towards certain tendencies.

One of the things I have been thinking about in relation to this is how speciations converge not through a matrix of identity ('the' animal, 'the' human), but through speeds and slownesses of welling co-constitutive ecologies. Thinking this way perhaps allows us to consider how fields of resonance, or what Simondon calls 'associated milieus', emerge not through identity structures (the human, the self) but through ecologies that are as much rhythms as 'beings' – different scales and intensities of time. This may in turn enable us to get beyond identity politics (as it continues to exist even within politics of affect) and explore the immanent coexistence of a relational third – what I have elsewhere called the interval. When the interval becomes an active part of what the event-constellation can do, we find ourselves in a 'radical empiricism' without a preconditioned sense of what the terms of the relation consist of. This, I think, is what we try to do with the SenseLab events and with our inquiries into new forms of collaboration. We ask: what does this third do? How does it speciate? What does it co-create? What kind of ecology is it?

I say this knowing that all speciations do culminate to some degree in species or categories. The point is not that there is no identity – no human, no animal, no plant – but that the species is not where the process begins or ends. Our proposition is not to negate species or identity, but to become aware that the force of speciation, of collective individuation, happens in the interstices where the ecologies are still in active transformation. In my own terms I would say that what is made possible by this approach is an opportunity for a kind of choreographic thinking which I define not as the imposition of a choreographic score, but as the creation of tools that enable the mobile diagram of speciations to come to the fore – a kind of incipient diagrammatic praxis.

Brian Massumi: Yes, we're in affect, affect is not in us. It's not a subjective content of our human lives. It's the felt quality of a relational field that is always 'more-than', as Erin emphasizes in her writing – always more-than one, to cite one of her book titles,[5] and always more-than human. Going back to the question of technique, the techniques have to be techniques of immanence – welling up from within that more-than of ourselves. It can't be otherwise, because you're in a situation of uncertainty, you don't have an overview, there's no position of mastery, there's a complexity and diversity in the field that you can't possibly comprehend completely, and you're changing with it. Because of this, the approach has to be heuristic and experimental, taking off from very partial points of entry where a tweaking might potentially amplify or resonate throughout the field. But you never know for sure. So you have to remain attuned, you have to keep attuned to how the field is affecting you, even as you are affecting it. So it's a kind of double becoming, where you as an individual are being modulated by the collective field, as much as the field is being modulated by your gestures. You're never standing outside just directing or judging or critiquing or commenting upon or describing. You're adventuring. You're taking risks, not so much in the sense of putting others at risk – although that could happen, which makes all of this directly a question of ethics – but more fundamentally taking risks with who you think and feel you are and what you can become.

[5] Erin Manning, *Always More Than One: Individuation's Dance* (Durham, NC: Duke University Press, 2013).

Erin Manning: I'm thinking of one example. I've been doing a lot of work with autistics. Many of them explicitly think of themselves as an ecological field, or a speciation as I described it earlier. Tito Mukhopadhyay explains that this has to do with a sense of bodying which extends the feeling of self into the environment. He, like many autistics, has no real sense of where his body begins and ends (he speaks of flapping his arms in order to get a better sense of where his physical body exists in space). We also see this tendency of an ecological 'bodying' in young children where the limits between body and world are blurred. Brian told me a story about when his son Jesse was little: if he got hurt and Brian said 'where does it hurt', Jesse would point not to his body but at the ground where he fell. Sequestering the hurt to the body as we do when we grow up and learn how to distinguish the world from the body actually simplifies the ecology of the event. Because obviously the hurt – knee meets ground – makes no sense outside that event and can't really be distinguished from it: it is a speciation, a resonant ecology that has pain as its time-signature but lives somewhere between body and world. This foregrounding of ecology over identity is something Mukhopadhyay talks about in wonderful terms in a book called *The Mind Tree*.[6] One of my favourite parts of the book is where he gives us the typical scenario between the autistic child and the doctor, but in his own terms. That scenario looks something like this: the parent brings a 'non-communicative' child to the doctor and explains that something went

[6] Tito Rajarshi Mukhopadhyay, *The Mind Tree* (New York: Arcade, 2011).

wrong around the age of two. Before that, the parent explains, the child progressed quite 'normally' and then the child began to 'lose' language. And then a whole bunch of behaviours began to stand out: tantrums, extreme physical discomfort which a parent might not understand or take as the child being difficult or being moody, a lack of eye contact, and a general sense often experienced by the parent that the child is no longer communicating. So the parent takes the child to a therapist or doctor, and the doctor begins to test the child. When the autistic child won't make eye contact, won't play etc., won't identify as such in relation to the doctor, the doctor says 'your child is unempathetic, unrelational, and really it's a cross to bear; I'm very sorry but you are facing a life-time of non-communication with your child'. Tito talks about his experience of this event, challenging the identity politics engrained in it and emphasizing another kind of encounter, one that is profoundly ecological and nonhuman-centred – he writes of going into the doctor's office and recalls the magical way the light reflected on the mirror and the way the mirror reflected back on the wall. He talks about how the curtains interacted with the light and how the door reflected it and how all this affected his relationship to the room and the room's relationship to him. And he writes that yes, the doctor did ask him to play with some toys on the table – but they weren't as interesting as the movements of the light so he chose not to play with them, or perhaps didn't really even acknowledge the doctor's request or the others in the room. Why would he? The movements of light were much more interesting. When at the end of that meeting the doctor told his mother that he was autistic Tito assumed not that he had a disability – what was disabling about this wonderful game of perception he had been playing? – but that all the non-speaking moving things in his life were in fact also autistic – the curtains, the fan. What great company!

Tito uses this story to explain that there is no lack of communication here, no lack of empathy – but rather a kind of hyper-relationality that does not settle for the human as its point of focus. He emphasizes that in the doctor's office he was very much part of the welling speciation room-light-movement, and that this speciation was very much intertwined with an emergent relational field in which he was intensively active. The suggestion becomes: we, 'neurotypicals', are so busy looking for human–human modes of communication that we too often overlook these emergent ecologies. In addition, we place identity politics and empathy on the same level and assume that communication is limited to human–human interaction. In doing so, we negate the force of the radically empirical and dismiss the myriad speciations in our midst.

Brian Massumi: This connects in many ways with what I have been working on. Rather than separating out two types of experience, then calling one normal and the other not, what Erin was just saying moves towards an ecology of experiences where there is not only diversity but overlap. What she was just describing as an autistic experience or autistic mode of perception has a lot in common with that emergent level of immediation I was discussing earlier. The example of the knee and the ground is a really good one. When I asked my son Jesse where it hurt and he pointed at the ground, he wasn't just pointing to a place, he was pointing to the event. At that age, children haven't learned yet to locate pain in the conventional way, as a feeling separate from the event. The event has factors that we later come to locate as 'out there' as well as 'in here', so at the emergent level of immediation, the pain spans that difference. At that level, its significance is also not entirely defined. No child can ignore it, so it comes immediately with significance, but how much? What kind? Is this the kind of hurt it's acceptable to cry about? The child will often look to the parent for a cue before following up on the pain with a cry. What our pains become for us is a product of learning how to parse the event in acceptable ways, but it never entirely loses its relational, transindividual span. Each pain event starts back in the interval Erin was talking about – x meets y, in an as yet indeterminate welling, and what x and y will turn out to have been, coming out of that encounter, is always up for grabs to some extent. This is another illustration of the bracing into a relational field I was describing earlier.

Accidents are another example. As an accident is happening, time slows and we have this incredibly vivid sense of everything coming immediately together – light reflections suspended in the air, floating shards of glass, the sound of screeching tyres stretched out as if by a synthesizer, an infinity of details. It's only later that what autistics call the 'chunking' into separate objects, factors and phases of the event occurs. And that's all learned. There are techniques for that. An unexpected event throws everything into the air, brings all of life's aspects back into question. It's what I call shock. But as Walter Benjamin said, it's happening all the time in small ways. Something as simple as a shift in attention, even a blink, is a kind of microshock that forces us to re-establish focus, re-jig our potential actions, refresh our relational field – re-chunk. We're constantly re-generating experience out of these interruptions, big and small. We're a correlated population of intervals. As Erin says in her book *Always More Than One*, every experience we have starts anew from what she calls the autistic field of experience, or what I call the relational field in *Semblance and Event*. Her point is that all of us are on the continuum, we're all on the spectrum, but some of us, those whom the autistics call neurotypical, chunk so habitually that they forget the relational emergence of experience.

Bodil Marie Stavning Thomsen: And speaking of that, maybe we can return to the media-created affective level of immediacy as it occurs on a daily basis, in news on the screen, and in new media experiences generally. When you say that we are in the affect rather than affect being in us, it reminds me of Deleuze who says that we're in time, time is not in us. We have both of those experiences, both in it from both angles at the same time. What is interesting about new media experience is that it somehow returns to this experience, and frames it and makes it compelling as duration – or non-duration.

Brian Massumi: It seems to me that there's also a kind of ecology of time in the media environment. That article I wrote in *The Guardian* was quite a lesson for me because I had never written something journalistic like that, that goes online right away and gets an instant response. In academic publishing, it usually takes a year for something to get into print, and then it's another year or two before you get any response to it. Writing for online journalism was a very interesting experience. There were different media timelines that intersected around the posting of the article that had different affective tonalities and relational fields attached to them. There were the instantaneous reactions of the comments blog after the article. I'd say 99 per cent of the comments were not only negative, but absolutely vicious. After a few rounds, they weren't so much responding to the article as baiting each other. This led to a snowballing of derision and aggression. It lasted a couple of days, before the winds of derision subsided. What was ostensibly designed to be a public forum for considered discussion became a forum for fast and furious venting, for affective acting-out based on the presupposition that others' perceptions and opinions don't count – the farthest thing imaginable from the rosy image of the public sphere as a realm for sober deliberation, reflection and the concerned sharing of ideas. It's like that relational field was implanted with the presupposition that such a thing as a relational field does not exist, that everything comes down to personal feelings, and that expression is nothing more than venting them without regard. I think the public sphere – to the extent that such a thing ever existed, and I'm not convinced it did – is becoming more and more like that in all areas. The 'town halls' organized during the 2008 US presidential election had a similar ethos. But then, with *The Guardian* article, there were longer-duration timelines, in a different mode. These took the form of Facebook links and tweets, which operated with a presupposition of a relational field predicated on sharing and with an affective tonality of potential interest. The tweets disappear after their predetermined shelf life of two weeks. The Facebook links settle into the search engines, and can stay forever, like sediment from the event. Then there were the news aggregators that automatically sent the article out in all directions and embedded it in other sites, basically at random, and without any particular limit to how far afield it could go or long it would stay where it landed, enacting an ethos of trawling and grasping and appropriation endemic to the economy of internet content providers. So what was the media event of this little article? What was its relational field? It was all of those timelines, with their different modes of proliferation and differential attunements, embodying different ethoses of engagement. Even something as small as that tiny contribution to the internet far outpaced my personal ability to follow what became of it, and to understand how it was playing, because it was just too splayed out and proliferating. It was a weird feeling of instantly losing control over a product of your personal time investments and of the desire for them to yield a graspable result commensurate with your input, and on the same human scale. I was in that little event, I was in the splay, being pulled in all directions. I really didn't feel it as an experience I was having. It was like being drawn and quartered by an experience that had a life of its own and a time of its own – or multiple times – and that I was just the launch pad for it.

Erin Manning: I also wanted to draw attention to the fact that in your article you also talked about time in relation to the global media response. Fukishima had a turnover time, a life expectancy of about two weeks, if that, and then it was on to Libya. I found it interesting in terms of the time of media itself, which is actually very restricted if we're talking about how long the focus remains on an event. Then, as you say, there is this kind of viral level where the stories endlessly proliferate. Sometimes on Facebook I notice that old media stories are shared without the knowledge that they're old – this often happened in the recent Canadian election with people posting videos of prime minister Stephen Harper without realizing that these were already a few years old.

Brian Massumi: I call this new media ecology we're describing a 'quasi-public' sphere. I mean that there is relay and overlap between private and public messaging that blurs the boundaries between them. To continue with the Facebook example, you friend your friends' friends, and they friend yours, and soon you're sharing 'personal' news with total strangers. The mode of expression is still 'personal', but the presupposition is of a certain degree of publicness, more restricted than broadcast but not exactly intimate or personal in any way previous generations would have understood those words. I find this fascinating because this blurring of the boundaries of the public and the private isn't just the negative of them. It's a whole new relational field where the act of expression is already informed and formatted by its quasi-publicness, so that it is marked from within by the presence of others. It's an example of expression becoming explicitly what Deleuze and Guattari called a 'collective assemblage of enunciation'. To the extent that we produce ourselves through social media – in pretty much the same sense as when we refer to what film producers do – we are fairly explicitly participating in a collective individuation under the flimsy guise of the 'personal'.

Bodil Marie Stavning Thomsen: It's a situation that calls for a new affective politics. Perhaps it could be thought of in relation to what Marcel Mauss said about the structure of the gift. The gift is some way of attunement to another person or community, but it carries this possibility of iteration – you always have to re-give the gift in some sense. It's hard to say, but perhaps the media are actually enhancing that. The gift is in a way becoming bigger and bigger, but also becoming poisonous in some sense. So returning to this idea of eco-biological diagramming, in relation to affect, there's something to be done here. Something that has to do with value production. In a normal gift economy, everyone is acutely aware that it's a sharing, but that has been lost somehow, or blurred. You never know when the sharing stops or when it begins.

Erin Manning: Yes, the gift has become increasingly important to us, hence the framing of our most recent SenseLab event, 'Generating the Impossible' (2011), with the indigenous concept of potlatch.[7] I think that the native peoples who practise potlatch understand

[7] For an extended discussion of 'Generating the Impossible' and the 'Technologies of Lived Abstraction' series of Sense-Lab events of which it was a part, see Erin Manning and Brian Massumi, *Thought in the Act: Passages in the Ecology of Experience* (Minneapolis: University of Minnesota Press, 2014), part 2, pp. 83–151.

something very interesting about the way the gift is a creator of time. The gift is the gift of time. I take this to some degree from Derrida's reading of the gift –

Bodil Marie Stavning Thomsen: The pharmakon, or the remedy that is also a poison?

Erin Manning: There is a connection, but I'm thinking more of Derrida's book *Given Time* and his work on Marcel Mauss.[8] In the indigenous context, potlatch, the event of the gift, takes place in an attuning against war. The tribes come together. The potlatch is a ritual practice that shifts the stirrings of the war-machine towards something else. This something else is not about the object per se, not about material conditions alone. It is about shifting the field, and in the case of the potlatch this happens not only through the giving, but also through the destruction of the gift. It is about the ritual, the field of relation in-act, and not about the actual thing in itself. In the context of the SenseLab, this idea of the gift of time – what is given, what is destroyed, what is left over from the destruction – is central to our thinking as regards strategies for collective practice. We are continuously searching for techniques that allow us to foreground this opening of the event onto its own forces for giving time – giving time for exploration, giving time for failure. Failure – like the destruction of the gift in the potlatch – is important to us precisely because it frees the event towards the unknowable, causing the event to reattune to the conditions at hand.

[8] Jacques Derrida, *Given Time*, trans. Peggy Kamuf (Chicago: University of Chicago Press, 1994).

For 'Generating the Impossible', one of the potlatch techniques we conceived of was that of the 'free radical', which we initially defined – with the assistance of Australian artist Paul Gazzola – as a generator of intervals. The free radical would in some sense be what is everywhere activated in the event. But in this case, it would also take the form of this singular individual, Paul Gazzola, and we would experiment with what this technique might produce. This technique came to us through thinking of the gift itself as a free radical – that which activates a modality of attunement where the field is both sustained and destabilized, done and undone, by what goes into it. The free radical in biology is a molecule that is necessary for metabolism, but that can also damage tissue – so a pharmakon of sorts. The task of the free radical was to help crystallize emergent collectivities of affective attunement, but also to disrupt them if they became too harmonious and started to settle into in-groups. A kind of trickster figure. In the end, I think it turned out to be a very interesting way to intervene in and move with the event. We collectively did eventually realize that the force of the free radical was based on our collective capacity to activate it everywhere in the shifting event-field. But it was useful for us to have it embodied in the first instance so we wouldn't lose sight of it. This became a technique for conceiving of the potential of collective individuation to produce ecologies of experience that at once sustain it and reopen it to its potential. I should emphasize that our events are never created out of an 'everything goes' sensibility. They are crafted through experimentations with a structured improvisation that we hope can activate potential paths for collective exploration. So when I speak about what is left over, I am really speaking of excavating from the event its force towards the as-yet unthought or unformed. That this can fail is clear – and the failure then becomes another way of restarting, of participating, if possible, in a new kind of event-time.

The question, it seems to me, is always 'where do we go from here?' And how can the 'here' be tweaked without our thinking that everything begins with us, with the human, with the personal? How can emerging ecologies attune such that they can produce different affects? How can we conceive of enabling constraints for such an attunement to become part of how event-time expresses itself? We think a lot about the modulation of effects – how can the event carry the force of uncertainty without breaking into compensatory nodes of self-consciousness? How can the collective recompose without an imposition of a pre-established system for the ordering of the disparate? And of course we fail and fail. But what emerges nonetheless is a strong collective sense, I think, that it is key to move the issue from human centredness to that of speciation, or an ecology of practices. To move from the personal to a sense of event response-ability. With this approach the question of responsibility, the ability to respond, is never before the event. Working collectively from this vantage point asks us not to put ourselves in a pre-planned position of benevolence or generosity or accommodation as though there were an outside of the event. Rather, it pushes us to develop ways of conceiving of event-generosity – where it is the event that creates conditions for its own potential openings. Of course this way of operating can be construed as extremely dangerous: we cannot know what the event can do before it is doing it, before it is doing us. The event itself is a free radical in a larger ecology. But we believe this is a risk worth taking since we cannot risk not taking it. The gift is in the giving, with the event as gift-giver, and what resolves from there is always to be determined.

Brian Massumi: Yes, and when we were initially thinking about the gift and the gift economy of the potlatch – we talked about it last year when we were in Denmark, a year before 'Generating the Impossible' – we were captivated by passages in *A Thousand Plateaus* that discuss an alternative conception of how economy works and what values an economy produces.[9] Deleuze and Guattari say that what's at stake in the economy is the relational field. What sustains an economy isn't so much its structure – the pre-established order of identified positions or social roles proposed for individuals. What they say is that what's at stake is how the limits and thresholds of the field play out. Deleuze and Guattari develop a concept of the limit as organizing the relational field, borrowing from marginalist economics but giving it a twist of their own. A relational field is unlimited in the sense that it is full of unactualized potential for value creation, both economic and affective, and for the generation of events and of novelty. But at the same time a relational field is limited in the sense that there are certain points beyond which it does not go. There are thresholds beyond which it flips into a

[9] Gilles Deleuze and Félix Guattari, *A Thousand Plateaus* (Minneapolis: University of Minnesota Press, 1987), pp. 437–40.

qualitatively different field of relation. They give the example of a tribal society and the production of axes for working the earth. If the production of axes goes beyond a certain quantity, the surplus is apt to be absorbed by another activity – fighting, for example. This might lead to a shift from limited ritual warfare to a new organization of war. This in turn might lead to social stratification around a new kind of warrior caste. The entire nature of the society will change. So there's a quantitative threshold that coincides with a qualitative tipping point. The qualitative aspect is what really counts. Quantitative accumulation within the usual bounds is just more of the same. Their point is that the quantitative aspect of an economy, which we tend to think is what economics is all about, is doubled by a qualitative order, and that's where the real, processual differences lie. When a threshold is crossed into a new relational field, everything re-jigs, what is valued in life changes, life is revalued.

Fundamentally, economies are qualitative economies of life-value, and the quantitative aspect is an index of that. Deleuze and Guattari say that there is an intuitive collective understanding of where the limits are for a given field. Not going past the limit, avoiding tumbling over into a new field, is a marker of people's collective, affective investment, their differential attunement, towards staying in the relational field they're in, not because of how much they get per se, but because of the life-values, the quality of life, that this relational field affords them. This is not of course a consensus. It can be a highly complex dynamic including opposing forces. In fact, the more complex the relational field, the more contested its limits and thresholds are. Deleuze and

Guattari's point is that not moving over into a new field, not enabling or effecting a tip-over, is basically a collective decision involving affective evaluations that have to do with purely qualitative, integrally relational values. Those evaluations are not necessarily wholly conscious, or available for reflective judgement. In fact, it is certain that they are not, because of the points we've been making throughout this interview about how movement in a relational field by nature overspills the individual and its actuality. That is why affective politics are so necessary, and why they have to be directly collective. The challenge is how to practise an affective politics that is capable of addressing the nonconscious dynamics, that occurs on an affective level of immediation, and how to do that without becoming coercive. It's in response to that problem that at the SenseLab we have been exploring concepts like technique of relation, gift, tweaking and modulation, conviviality, processual proposition, and lure. And we're doing this within the wider perspective of anti-capitalist struggles. The marginalist logic of the limit, as reconceptualized by Deleuze and Guattari, applies just as much to the capitalist economy as to a tribal economy. For example, effectively addressing underemployment and exploitation, or addressing the ecologically disastrous capitalist imperative of endless growth, or truly addressing the innate tendency within a capitalist economy for inequalities to grow, and grow more and more intractable, could well lead towards threshold states. What does an anti-capitalist affective politics look like that moves the global relational field in other directions? All I can say is that to improvise that kind of politics we have to take seriously the qualitative-relational workings of the field we're in, we have to accept our immersion in it, and see ourselves as working immanently to that field, and work to move it from within towards one of its constitutive limits and over the tipping point.

Jonas Fritsch: In our preparatory readings for 'Generating the Impossible', and in the whole spirit of this summer's event, there was a central concern for the notion of life and bringing into existence, for the new modes of existence that Guattari talks about. For Deleuze, too, in his Spinoza book, it's about generating different manners of living as an end in itself. Erin, you talked about a project for 'life-living'...

Erin Manning: Yes, a force for life that extends beyond this human life to the life of organic–inorganic ecologies or speciations – a different way of conceiving of life. I often come at this through Deleuze's last article, 'Immanence: A Life',[10] which, it seems to me, gives us profound tools for beginning to think life-living not in terms of 'this life' but as a project for *a* 'life' differently conceived, life as an ecology of practices that continuously interfolds the inorganic with the organic, the human and the nonhuman, shaping experience in the making.

Brian Massumi: When we talk about value, life and affirming relational intensities of experience, it's often

[10] Gilles Deleuze, 'Immanence: A Life', in *Two Regimes of Madness: Texts and Interviews 1975–1995*, ed. David Lapoujade, trans. Ames Hodges and Mike Taormina (New York: Semiotext(e), 2007), pp. 388–93.

misunderstood as a celebration of good feeling, good vibes, but that's not what it's about. If you want to remodulate relational potentials that overspill the present, you have to in a sense dilate that moment. You have to suspend the 'chunking', suspend the crystallizing of pragmatic presuppositions and the precipitous launching into the most prepared and accessible action paths. This involves a certain amount of disorientation, and that can be painful. Even so, it's still a joy of a kind, because it's intense, it's vital. In *Always More Than One*, Erin calls that intensity of the suspense of a relational modulation under way 'enthusiasm'. It's the feeling of vitality that belongs to the relational field. It belongs to individuals only to the degree that they are braced into that field, in differential attunement to its stirring towards movement – its 'preacceleration' as Erin says – to the potential making itself felt in it. It isn't only attached to what we think of as positive emotions. It's more an intensity of movement, and of processual attention. Raymond Ruyer calls it 'enthusiasm of the body', and associates it with play. Our whole being is in it, body and thought, together towards movement. In *Semblance and Event*, I write of this in terms of 'vitality affect', borrowing a term from Daniel Stern (which is also where 'affective attunement' comes from), and I call the relational in-bracing it coincides with 'bare activity'. These are all ways of working through the concept of 'a' life as Erin takes it up.

Erin Manning: For us the free radical might be thought in tandem with the concept of 'a' life, or the 'preindividual' in Simondon. The preindividual does not connote something that precedes a process of individuation. It is, rather, an accompanying share of the process, a virtual contribution, you might say, that is capable of touching on the more-than of experience. We wondered whether the free radical might similarly be capable of making felt this share of the more-than that is so difficult to encapsulate but so central to the development of new forms of thought and collaboration. Life-living is one way of articulating this share that coincides with 'this' life, but isn't reducible to it, because it also includes the process of life, in its preacceleration. Life-living is the virtual force of a process that creates us.

Bodil Marie Stavning Thomsen: But in the event you have the ability to actually experience it.

Erin Manning: I think so, yes. I don't know if you've seen Ari Folman's film *Waltz with Bashir* (2008)? It's a film I write about in *Always More Than One*. I am thinking of it here in terms of this virtual share of experience that can be made felt but isn't actualized as such. When I was writing about the film, I knew that *Waltz with Bashir* was a film that was received quite badly by a number of left-wing academics in Israel and elsewhere, who criticized it for once more placing the Israeli experience at the centre, thus making it all about Israeli suffering. I read it differently, though, focused as I was on the way life was portrayed, and especially this aspect of the preindividual. The question for me was how life can persist, or what form life can take after a horror such as the Sabra and Shatila massacre. One answer to this would be to place everything into humanist terms. This, I argue, is what Levinas does when he goes to Israel shortly after the massacre and proclaims that there are times when we cannot face the neighbour, that sometimes there are enemies, pure and simple. I argue that at crucial moments a humanist ethics tends to fall back into the most simplistic differentiation of self and other, friend and enemy – an identity politics – even when its aim is complex, as Levinas's surely is. What *Waltz with Bashir* does, I suggest, is take us elsewhere, away from a humanist identity politics to a different kind of politics, altogether different – one that troubles the very notion of the centrality of the face-to-face encounter – to ask us how the horror of the other's face catapults us into an affective turn that destabilizes the very idea of 'positioning' that a politics of recognition presupposes. What *Waltz with Bashir* does that is so powerful – and it does this through the movement of the image, the intensity of colour and sound, as much as or even more than through the narrative – is provoke another way of engaging with the as-yet-unthinkable (or as-yet-unfaceable). One of the ways it does this is by continuously disengaging affect from the face of the human – the human face moves from shot to shot in an expressionless sameness. What is active in the film is another kind of affective politics, one, as Brian might say, of bare activity – a welling of experience in the making. What's important to me here is that we find ways of conceiving of a complex politics that moves beyond humanism towards a concept of life that troubles categories we too often feel are predetermined. This leads, perhaps, to a more complex notion of coexistence.

What I am proposing with *Waltz with Bashir* is similar to how I approached Leni Riefenstahl's films in my book

Relationscapes.[11] We can learn, I think, from the complex modalities at work beyond narrative structures, even in a case like Riefenstahl where the explicit politics is so odious to us. In Riefenstahl, as in Folman, what appears are 'biograms' – forces for bodies in the making – what I call 'bodyings'. The biograms themselves are not inflected with an extrinsically assigned value. Their value is intrinsic to their operation. It is their force to make felt how bodyings are propagated. In the case of both these film makers, the bodyings are always speciations in the sense we were talking about before – ecologies of expression that drive becoming, rather than structures of identity. In the Riefenstahl example, I've argued that the biogram in her films tends towards kinds of fascist becomings that are more creative – and in a way more dangerous – than the ones we associate overall with Hitlerism. They are more dangerous, because far less disciplinary, as Foucault might say. In the Folman example a different kind of bodying is at work which also has certain fascist tendencies (as all micropolitics do). But at the same time, it proposes a different way of 'facing' the question of the human share in existence. What I take away from both of these examples is that politics is not generalizable – that the event (be it in a film or in collective action) creates its own stakes, its own limits and potential tipping points. We must continuously be alert to these stakes and engage with the limits. Ari Folman takes an important risk, I feel, in staging the encounter in such complex terms without pre-defining the friend and the enemy.

[11] Erin Manning, *Relationscapes: Movement, Art, Philosophy* (Cambridge, MA: MIT Press, 2009).

In so doing, he forces the unthinkable upon us and involves us in the process of fashioning a politics to come that will always have to invent its own limits, and trouble them.

I think that the biggest mistake we make is to pretend that we can categorize and compartmentalize events according to pre-established criteria. This is just too clean. I think that art can do the work of keeping experience complex by creating an open field for thought in the making. All open fields eventually get captured in all kinds of ways, but this capture does not negate the trace of the process of life-living.

5

Immediation

With
Erin Manning

Christoph Brunner*: An issue that has been coming up a lot recently regarding affect, in the European and especially German-speaking academic environment, concerns the question of what the politics of affect might be, specifically if you think about affect in relation to immediacy. The critique I often hear is that affect-oriented approaches tend to focus on the immediate without considering the historical background and the ways in which mediating frames of reference are constructed. I feel that it is very

* Interview by Christoph Brunner (2013)

important to contextualize the notion of experience which needs to be addressed in relation to affect and immediacy.

Brian Massumi: Immediation does not exclude determinations from the past or tendings towards the future. The term 'immediation' is a way of drawing attention to the event as the primary unit of the real. The idea is that whatever is real makes itself felt in some way, and whatever makes itself felt has done so as part of an event. It has entered in some way into the immediacy of the moment as a factor in the event now taking place. This means, paradoxically, that whatever of the past is going to count in this event has to presentify itself. The first stage of an event of experience, according to Whitehead, is one of re-enaction, which I often call 'reactivation'. Whitehead makes it very clear that this inaugural phase of presentification is affective. It's a direct, unmediated feeling of what past events have left in the world for the coming event to take up as its own potential. This cannot be consciously discriminated as yet, because the event is just beginning and hasn't sorted out what it will become yet. It can only be felt. But since the feeling is of potential, it can already be construed as a kind of thinking forward. It's a thinking-feeling in the immediacy of what's coming. Immediacy, in this way of thinking about it, is always in relation to the past, but it's a direct, unmediated relation to the past as the past is coming back to life in the singularity of a given situation that hasn't yet fully played itself out. There is no general reference to the past. There's a singular inclusion of the past in oncoming activity. Immediation is actually more intensively inclusive of the past than a reflective or critical thinking about it, because it includes the *force* of the past – where it is potentially heading beyond itself, as a function of its own momentum meeting the singularity of a new arising. Immediation is the past bumping against the future in the present.

Erin Manning: Affect is a way to account for experience in its in-forming. In both our writing and in the work at the SenseLab, Brian and I often focus on affect because our concern is with how emergent experience composes in ways that are proto-political. Our recent emphasis on immediation comes out of this concern. As you know, given that you're a participant in the new project phase at the SenseLab which we've called 'Immediations', we are interested in drawing attention to how the stakes of experience occur in the immediate interstices of its coming to be. As Brian emphasizes, this coming to be does not in any way rule out the force of pastness. In fact, one of the things immediation as a concept does is emphasize the nonlinearity of the time of the event, or what I sometimes call event-time. Event-time emphasizes time's affective force, in the event. This affective force is laden with both pastness and futurity, but in a way that is singularly active in the now of experience.

Christoph Brunner: In a recent interview [see chapter 4] you talk about the affective field generating an immediate in-bracing of multiple bodies in an event and in differential attunement. In that interview, you point out that any concept becomes problematic if we use it to try to generate new universals.

Immediation

Erin Manning: What interests me in particular is how fields of relation agitate and activate to emerge into what I think of as collectivities. I don't mean human collectivities but ecological environments that include the human in its co-composing with the nonhuman. This is what I call the 'more-than-human'. To account for those emergent fields you need a vocabulary that touches on what Brian was talking about in his reference to pastness within immediation as 'a thinking-feeling in the immediacy of what's coming'. Whitehead calls this non-sensuous perception, emphasizing that it is essential that we understand that there is a phase of experience previous to sensory experience that is capable of accounting for how the event immanently co-composes with pastnesses in the act. Experience in this phase is non-sensuous, according to Whitehead. The force of the past that is presenting itself cannot present itself in sense-perception, for the obvious reason that the sense-perceptions belonging to the past are in the past and stay there. The reason why this is so important to me is because the privileging of sense-perception tends to lead us directly to human subjectivity – to a subjective notion of memory as founding human subjectivity. If we begin there, with the subject, with sensuous perception, with subjective memory, we begin much later in the account. Rather than seeing how the immanent event creates an emergent ecology, and then becoming interested in what this emergent ecology can do (how it expresses itself, how it is proto-political etc.), we take the human as a given and ask what it is doing in the event. This places the event at the mercy of the human, rather than placing the human as part of the ecology of the event. If we do the second, we are in a complex array of experience in which the human is one among many. Or, more precisely, where there is no 'easy' category, such as 'human', to begin with. This second approach, which we are here linking to immediation, requires a different kind of work because it does not lay out, yet, the stakes of the emergent collectivity. For me the question of 'how it comes into formation' is really the political question, which is not to disparage an account that comes from another perspective, which would be a historical account of already emerged political formations, for instance. I just don't think that the force of the political in its potential for change occurs at that level.

Brian Massumi: From my point of view, in current discussions of affect there is often a misunderstanding of what is at stake. The gesture of encapsulating it in an 'affective turn', as opposed to the preceding 'linguistic turn' or any other sort of turn, assumes that affect is a thing, something that can be separated from other things, like you would put a fork on one side of your plate and the spoon on the other, and then position yourself polemically according to whether you think it's better to scoop or stab your food. It's a bit Swiftian, like arguing about which end of the egg to open. When you define affect as Spinoza does, as an ability to affect or be affected, it's clear that it's a dimension of all activity, whether we see fit to categorize that activity as subjective or objective. It is just as obvious that there is an affective dimension to language. Affect is already on the plate, whatever your preferred intellectual diet, and it lends itself to many kinds of utensils. The point of insisting on the necessity of taking affect into account is not to say that we should think about affect instead of language, or pay attention only to the infra-subjective and infra-objective germinal stirrings of events that Erin was just talking about and forget about subjects or objects. It's just not an either-or. It's a question of differing modes of activities that factor into events. The concept of affect, as taken up in a philosophy of immediation, is a way of focusing on the germinal modes of activity that factor into events as they are just beginning, and are not yet fully determined as to where they might lead. It's a directly relational concept, because you have to think the 'to affect' and 'to be affected' as two sides of the same coin of the event. Affect is a point of entry into an eventful, relational field of complexity that is already active, and still open-ended. The point of thinking with affect is to think through our implication in relational fields, and the potential we might find there. There is no general model of affect. The way the past carries over into the new event, which tendencies are reactivated, in what mix and with what formative interactions, all of that is completely singular to the situation, so the theory of affect has to be custom tailored to every field of event-formation, and even to every event. It has to be continually reinvented.

Christoph Brunner: Brian, this leads me to your exposition of bare activity and Erin's notion of the in-act. In thinking about the question of activity or the act, there is a tendency to assume that they are only concerned with emergence. But there is also Whitehead's concept of 'perishing', which you both take up in your work. I was wondering how can we think in three kinds of tonalities of activity: as bare activity, a worlding and force of life, continuation and renewing; then the act of formation of subjectivity and the kinds of inflections you can try to seek out, insert and inflect; and finally what Judith Butler calls 'supported action', underlining how there is a kind of material grounding of the vitalism of the body that needs to be sustained and supported. This last idea refers to the fact that new events are grounded in what past events that have 'perished' leave in the world for renewal. Some people might think that the politics, ethics and aesthetics of emergence have over-emphasized one end of the continuum, whereas we also need to include an ethics and aesthetics of perishing.

Erin Manning: This is an important point. I think we have to dissociate Brian's ideas of bare activity, or my focus on the in-act, from the way activity is mobilized by capitalism. Bare activity has nothing to do with 'doing something' in the sense of that capitalist busy-ness. As Brian often says, its not doing something, it's 'something doing', emphasizing, as I did earlier, how the event's own coming into act is what is at stake, not only the human subject's activity in the event. Something doing is never limited to human doing: it asks instead how the doing effects the field of relations active in the event. Some of the effects are definitely human effects, but these are always in a constellation that is more-than human. Activity is therefore never reduced to what the human does, as tends to be the case in work that criti-cizes action as a concept (such as Bifo's [Franco Berar-di's] account of activism, for instance). It has to do instead with the generative potential of ecologies in their coming to be an event.

Whitehead's book *The Function of Reason* is very interesting in relation to activity and life.[1] The question that Whitehead raises in it is the question of the quality of life. He asks, what is it that can account for the fact that we strive to live well rather than simply living? This question is not strictly directed to the human, but to the way appetition functions in the ecology of practices of which humans are but one aspect. Creativity is at the heart of Whitehead's analysis. For Whitehead, one of the ways ecologies evolve towards complexity is through their appetition for the more-than of experience: they have a concern for how the doing happens, how the something-doing connects to other something-doings to generate modes of existence that are novel. Whitehead's concept of the novel is not the capitalist concept that emphasizes the importance of the 'newest new'. Creativity here refers to the generation of new forms of value that give rise to new forms of life. This is an account of valuation in the Nietzschean sense: it challenges the notion of evaluation according to external criteria with the idea that how an event comes into itself is a mode of valuation in itself. Any actual occasion for Whitehead is a mode of valuation: the question is, how does the event value its own mode of existence, how does it enjoy its own existence?

Brian Massumi: Going back to the notion of activity, for us it's not about instrumental activity. We're not talking about work, activity as it is captured and organized by the capitalist system. The activations and

[1] Alfred North Whitehead, *The Function of Reason* (Boston: Beacon Press, 1958).

reactivations we're talking about happen at a very different level. It's simply the idea that whenever something comes visibly or palpably to expression, it is emerging not out of nowhere, and not out of the structure of the past as fully determining, but out of a background activity that is inheriting from the past but also creating the conditions for what will come next that will supersede the past and perhaps change the nature of what comes of it. Activity is not grounded in substance or in essence. It's grounded in prior activity, taking a new twist. That's the basic tenet of what I call 'activist philosophy', which I see as a complement to an immediations approach. Every time there is a thought, there has already been activity in the body. Every time there has been activity in the body, there has been activity in the environment. There are interlinkings of different levels of activity channelled into certain points of more or less clear expression. It is at the points of more or less clear expression that activity in this primary sense can be captured by apparatuses like those of capitalism, and converted into work. It is also at those points of clear expression that emergence is coming to the end of its arc. The movement of expression is culminating. The event 'perishes'. The potentials it carried to expression are then ready for reactivation, either as conditions for a new emergence, or as captured potentials feeding a self-perpetuating structure that has found ways of reactivating itself across the perishings of events. Emergence and perishing are not opposites. They are pulses or phases in a process. An emergence lives on its own becoming. As soon as it expands its potential for that becoming, it perishes. If there is apparent continuity – even at the level of a rock, as the power of persistence of a rock – it's because a capability has set in to regenerate the same form across the perishings, so that the next emergence is more similar to than different from the last. Whitehead says this very clearly: a rock is an accomplishment. Something from the past creates conditions of conformity for the next emergence, and it is the reuptake of these by the new occasion which accounts for the continuity of lines of existence. Whitehead defines re-enaction as it is in conformity to the past as the 'physical pole' of events. He defines the 'mental pole' of events as what introduces novelty into the re-enaction, and jumps ahead from there. Fundamentally, that means appetition, as Erin was just discussing – the singularizing force of futurity. It is crucial to realize that the mental pole as Whitehead defines it has nothing to do in the first instance with human thought or subjectivity. You have to think the emergence and the perishing, the conformal persistence and rearising, the cut of the new and the continuity, the physical and the mental, together, as mutually imbricated modes of process. As phases of process they are always interlinked, and are found to one degree or another in every event at any level of existence.

On the question of effectiveness. When we talk about effectiveness, we're usually thinking about what philosophers call efficient causality. It's the idea that an effect is directly proportionate to its cause, that the cause can be isolated from background activity, and then connected in linear fashion to its effect. It's basically the billiard-ball model, where the future is completely determined by a measurable force that is transmitted from the past through a part-to-part connection, in a localized impact. It's the model of work again, but in the physics sense of the term. And this kind of causality, precisely, corresponds to Whitehead's physical pole (which is not, however, reducible just to that). The mental pole is also effective – in introducing novelty. This complicates things, because when novelty happens, the unfolding of the event has not been linear. It has been inflected. Where does the nonlinearity come from? It comes from what is not completely determined in the field of relations. It comes from the background activity conditioning the event's emergence. It comes from the complexity of relations, from interference and resonance effects between the formative factors entering into play. There is always a margin of play in an event due to the complexity. This happens directly on the relational level, not part-to-part. It's not closed or linear enough to be called causality. 'Conditioning' has to be distinguished as a mode of effectiveness in its own right, as distinct from causality. Both modes of effectiveness, of course, are active in every event, and a large part of what makes for the singularity of an event is how they shake down in relation to each other.

Erin Manning: I am wondering how we can move this discussion towards a few examples, since what you're talking about, Brian, happens in all kinds of everyday situations. We could give ourselves as a challenge to make a list of the ways in which we habitually believe we can will the organization, or the outcome, or the effectiveness of a given situation. In doing so, we would realize that it is not the outcome which we control, but

the habit of how we believe we can control it! The habit
of entering into a process brings with it the promise that
a process engaging with the same conditions twice can
generate an event that looks like the event that it generated the first time. But what Brian is saying is that if
you take this process seriously, and attend to how it
evolves in each of its phases, you will find that no event
can be mapped in advance. The event takes us with it
and the outcome is always experienced in retrospect:
ah! that's what it was! But instead of saying 'that's what
it was!' we have the habit of taking the past and imposing it on the future, quietly exclaiming 'that's what it
will be!' Immediation tries to challenge that habit.

What we have found in our collective SenseLab
network as we work through the relationship between
philosophy, art and activism is that techniques have to
be generated in the event, each occasion anew, because
if they are not, they simply don't work. That's the pragmatic side or as we call it the speculative pragmatic side.
The event generates its own forms of speculation and
forms of pragmatism, and you have to be in the event
to compose with them. This is a relational task at the
level of the field itself. If you think of yourself as the
subject of the event, you'll fail simply because you will
have taken yourself out of all of those complex relational tendencies of the event to generate its own potential. What is at stake here is understanding not the
agency of the subject, but the *agencement* of the event
in its speculatively pragmatic unfolding. This is a word
that is impossible to translate. The best that anyone's
come up with is 'assemblage', but that's misleading.
Agencement connotes a doing doing itself. You have to
understand the event itself as agency-ing.

Brian Massumi: You can think of any example where you are in the situation where there is a power relationship. It is very clear, if you're a professor and walk into a classroom, that you are immediately in a power situation over the students. You can basically make them do what you want. You can tell them to give you a fifteen-page paper by a certain date and they do it or suffer certain consequences. The only reason that I have the power over them is because we are co-implicated in a situation that draws on certain institutional structures, and we have acquired the adaptive habits and skills they assume and produce. When I say that I have power, it is actually self-aggrandizing, because what I have is only the power to activate certain constraints and forces that are embedded in the relational field. When I act I am more of a catalyst for the reactivation of those forces than a direct commander or autonomous willer. That's always the case, to one degree or another. Our freedom doesn't consist in making a choice or decision that comes only out of our own subjectivity – in other words, out of nowhere. Our freedom is how we play our implication in the field, what events we succeed in catalysng in it that bring out the latent singularity of the situation, how we inflect for novel emergences. That is a relational question, because it doesn't happen part-to-part in billiard-ball fashion. If how you're inflecting the event doesn't resonate or interfere with everyone present, and affect all the formative factors integrally, the conformal forces that are ready and waiting in the situation are going to have the upper hand.

Christoph Brunner: That's an interesting point. I have been re-reading Simondon recently, and Muriel Combes's book on his work.[2] Both address the question of anxiety. It seems to me that at the core the question of anxiety concerns different modes of resonance, and what you can create through the openness of a situation. On the one hand, this requires us to think about what means and techniques there are to become a catalyst and to benefit from surfing that wave, as Deleuze would say. On the other hand, it makes us think about the moment of impasse where everything seems to be locked and gridded. As Simondon says, that's the moment of anxiety and death. This leads me to think about the process of bifurcation in a life-practice – what kinds of techniques can be used for nurturing, and where you go from there. Thinking about the practices of research-creation we have been working on for a while at the SenseLab – investigating how to work, act, think, write and move in the immediacy of an event, and how to create something from there that comes into its own, singularizing and resonating-with, so as to renew the event. As part of this investigation, we ask what kinds of metastable fields can be constituted. How do we create dense fields that modulate in a way that is all their own? However, some of these fields and modulations generate more lures, open up more potential, for subsequent take-up in different contexts than others do.

Brian Massumi: Simondon's concept of anxiety is clearly in dialogue with existentialist and existential phenomenological thinking. It's a response to the anxiety

[2] Muriel Combes, *Gilbert Simondon and the Philosophy of the Transindividual*, trans. Thomas Lamarre (Cambridge, MA: MIT Press, 2013).

attached to Heidegger's being-towards-death, and to Sartre's prescription for absolute subjective freedom of decision in the face of anxiety. He's trying to save our anxieties from either fate. For Simondon, anxiety has to do with the 'more than oneness' at the heart of the individual. This is basically the active, relational field of potential we've been talking about – what Erin's been calling the more-than. Simondon calls it the 'preindividual field' because it is what the individualized subject emerges, and re-emerges, from. Anxiety is created, according to Simondon, when this open-ended, formative field is mistaken for an interiority of the subject, rather than being recognized as the preindividual field from which the individual emerges as a subject. When the preindividual is mistaken for an interiority, the resulting subject feels that it should be able to hold all the potential of the field in itself. This is impossible, because as we were saying, the potential is irreducibly relational, and can only be held integrally in situations. It can't be accessed just by individual choice or decision, but only by events, in which others are also implicated. The imperative that the individual is often made to feel to live up to its own potential, mistaking the world's potential for a being-in-itself, creates an unliveable tension. It actually bottles the potential up. The other, in this account, is not the hell of our choices and decisions being limited by others, as it was for existentialism. The other is the outlet. The potential of the preindividual field is relational, and can only be expressed relationally, through and with others. In fact, Simondon defines the other in terms of that. He says that the perception of another is the perception of a perspective on the world. By that he doesn't mean a subjective point of view. It's an active perspective – ways of moving in the world, ways of catalysing events, ways of expressing, ways of changing with and through the inflections of events. If the other is an image of potential, then the multiplicity of others multiplies the potential, way beyond what one individual can hold in itself. All of that potential can only be got at if it is activated relationally. To think of it this way connects the preindividual to the transindividual. Experimenting in activating situational potentials pragmatically, in exploratory relational action, dissipates anxiety by reconnecting the preindividual to the transindividual. Again, freedom is not a question of the relation of the subject to itself. Freedom always comes out of active embeddedness in a complex relational field for the in-acting. One does not act freely. One acts freedom out.

Erin Manning: In that beautiful passage you and Brian were mentioning, Simondon also talks about solitude. He does this as part of an urgent call not to talk about tendencies like anxiety and even solitude in a way that reindividualizes them. They need to be thought of in the context of individuation, or the relational becoming of the individual. Reindividualizing is a temptation we have seen a lot these days. To bring anxiety, depression, panic back to the level of the individual. I think the work of Bifo is really exemplary in that way. I have recently been reading Bifo trying to understand the necessity and the urgency that he seems to feel in creating what I consider a repersonalizing account of experience that too often reindividualizes the question of anxiety. This reindividualization, which perhaps affects me most in the way Bifo combines his theory of the act with depression in his account of Guattari's so-called 'winter years', builds on his relation of friendship in ways that make me very uncomfortable.[3] In his account of Guattari, if I am very reductive, what we end up with is something like: 'I knew Guattari to have been depressed and therefore you must read Guattari's work as an activist, as a therapist, as a philosopher, in light of his depression.' This counters the in-act of Guattari's schizoanalytic practice – including his writing – in a fundamental way, it seems to me. Everything in Guattari, in my opinion, follows the lines of what Brian was just saying, working hard to understand the relationship between the preindividual, the transindividual and the group-subject. The question for Guattari is never reducible to the subject-position: it is always about creating and grasping new forms of subjectivity that emerge from the event. I have no doubt Guattari was depressed – but construing depression as counteracting the in-act simply makes no sense to me.

We are at a moment where collective action feels urgent to many of us. I don't know if we are at a moment that is less anxious or more anxious than other moments. What I do know is that an account of anxiety or depression has to be able to compose with the in-act in the way we are theorizing it here for it to align to a Guattarian way of thinking. The question of pathology and the therapeutic, when it comes up, has to be aligned to a Simondonian account of anxiety or solitude if we

[3] Franco Berardi (Bifo), *Félix Guattari: Thought, Friendship and Visionary Cartography*, trans. and ed. Giuseppina Mecchia and Charles J. Stivale (London: Palgrave Macmillan, 2008).

want to open it up beyond its reindividualizing tendencies. If this happens, the question of how the act produces new modes of existence will come up, and this will open up the exploration of neurodiversity in relation to the transindividual or the group-subject, as opposed to what Guattari, following Jean Oury, calls 'normopathy'.

Brian Massumi: I want to take up the notion of solitude you brought up in relation to anxiety in Simondon's work. I think that's really important too because when he talks about group-subjectivity or collective individuation, and the importance of entering into certain event-based actions in a relational field including others, people often think of it as this imperative of togetherness, to social transparency, and total availability to that interaction. I think what Simondon is trying to say with his concept of solitude is that if there is an imperative of that kind, it can be as limiting and painful as the anxiety of mistaking the preindividual for a subjective interiority. When he talks about isolation he is talking about an experience of transindividual potential, but in the absence of any particular acting-out of it. It's being in-acted; that is, felt actively, but in intensity. Deleuze says something very similar, and he is probably thinking of Simondon, when he says that even one person alone at their writing desk can be a collective. They can be in-acting a field of relational potential that would require a whole population to act out. They are in a very real sense a 'people to come'. Deleuze even suggests that this is where one is at one's most collective. The incitation to always communicate, the imperative to participate, the constant solicitation to interact can be an enslavement. It's becoming more and more part of the necessary work of capitalism. In the end, there's very little actually relational about it, in the emergent sense we've been talking about. Solitude can in fact be a relational antidote to that.

Erin Manning: In relation to the question of collective action, in the way we understand it at the SenseLab, we have been very influenced by Guattari's accounts of La Borde, the experimental clinic he worked at all of his life, and the ways in which it may be possible to compose across many different variations of solitude and anxiety – in ways that are not saying that two individuals compose face to face, but that the event as it is being generated allows for different compositions, transindividual compositions, infraindividual and preindividual compositions. One of our main concerns in terms of our activism has been creating techniques emergent within the group-subject to deal with burn-out, and with depression and anxiety when they come up. How do you manage health in ways that don't target the individual but engage with the milieu instead? This is a question we've discussed with our collaborators, the Boston-based Design Studio for Social Intervention, for whom in some ways this is even more urgent as they deal with very tough on-the-ground issues of racism and gang violence. Many of the collaborators and activists within the studio have lost family members to gang violence and they deal everyday with racism directed not only at them, but at the very question of what kinds of modes of existence exist for inner-city African-Americans in the US. They are completely committed to continuing to design what they call 'horizontal' practices to counter urban violence, but they are also often overwhelmed by the magnitude of the task. Anxiety and depression often come with burn-out. In the face of such adversity, it is difficult to sustain the field of relation generated by activist event practices, and prevent it from imploding under pressure. Techniques for avoiding or alleviating the implosion of course concern the individual, but they cannot be limited to him or her.

One thing we experiment with is the question of reconnecting affectively to the collective in a different way, getting away from thinking about 'being active' in the sense of 'doing something' and focusing instead on the in-act of 'something doing'. This brings us back to the earlier question of affect: what does it mean to co-compose? To co-compose is to allow for the possibility that we cannot know in advance where the collective value of our project resides. It means to become flexible in our understanding collectively of how value might eventually come to be understood. A collectivity in the way I understand it is always concerned with these speculatively pragmatic questions – speculative because they remain open to invention, pragmatic because they are born of a continual exploration of the in-act. At the SenseLab, one of the ways we move towards this question of collective value is through the concept of event-based care. Here I don't mean the subjectivity of human-to-human care, but rather how an event produces an environment that can sustain different kinds of participation which include different affective speeds, including the slownesses that we perhaps associate with depression, or the speeds we associate with anxiety. With event-care perhaps there is a kind of collective tending that comes close to the sense that Guattari gave to the word 'therapeutic'. Not therapeutic as individual therapy, but therapeutic in the sense of attending to how an event is capable of producing mutually imbricated modes of existence or modes of living which are sustainable in ways we can't yet imagine, and which produce new forms of life. I say this very tentatively as I am not at all certain that therapeutic is the right word for this.

Christoph Brunner: This is a very important point in relation to methods and the question the SenseLab always gets of what its methods are. If you move through a constant revaluation in the immediacy of an event happening, if you try to find ways not to do something *about* what's happening but rather to do in the happening, then you have to completely reconsider the way you use language. It also affects the way you inhabit the institutionalized field of academia, with its constraints and the closed systems we as academics have to work with and through while trying to sustain certain kinds of practices and shift and modulate other kinds of practices. Talking about 'techniques' and 'ecologies of practice' provides one way of undoing the claim for methods and appropriate instruments. Which leads me back to the language we work in, which is never just reducible to its established rules of usage. How can we conceive the language we use as part of our life practices – in the sense of thinking, living and writing in the presence of each other and in the presence of the many solitudes moving through us? What does it actually mean to undo the confined systems that create anxiety all over again? As an example, we could think of the 'Nonhuman Turn' conference we all attended last year in Milwaukee. I have never seen an academic event so full of anxiety. Especially among the PhD students, who are expected to do inventive work but didn't dare to speak up, to oppose or voice their concerns, for fear of stepping on someone's toes who might be on your future hiring committee.

Erin Manning: Brian and I have been very involved in this question over the last years. How does language also produce what Guattari would call an existential territory? I think that's what you are talking about – that traditional instrumental forms of generating so-called knowledge such as the conference are not very good at generating territories that aren't mimicking and reproducing the territory they have come out of. I mean they don't generate the new in that sense of a Whiteheadian co-composition. I was thinking about this issue recently in relation to an event we are having this fall called 'Enter Bioscleave' that will take place at Arakawa and Gins's experimental Bioscleave House on Long Island.[4] Last week Brian and I were in New York talking to Madeline Gins. All three of us are very engaged in the process of language – very interested in what language can do and particularly interested in its capacities as a concept-building practice to generate modes of existence. Sometimes we hesitate in our collaboration, however, since although our focus is often similar, our language can be quite different. Arakawa and Gins function on the basis of a procedural approach. Over a

[4] This event did not take place in the end due to Madeline Gins's illness.

period of thirty or forty years, they have defined a set of procedures that are both very firmly ensconced in their practice and very mobile, very rethinkable. These procedures are ecological at heart, but do operate from the perspective of what they call the 'organism that persons', thereby producing a perspectival approach that in many ways keeps the human at the centre of the inquiry (despite their openness to think across different forms of sentience).[5] We at the SenseLab have generated a set of techniques which are perhaps a bit different in their inflections because they have as their focus the ecology of the event. These approaches have a sister-hood and common interest and we know each other's work well. Yet, despite this, for four or five hours we were trying to understand each other's language. Not only to understand in a linguistic sense but to be able to mobilize its affective force. What was really genera-tive in this conversation was that Madeline wanted to figure out how to proceduralize our techniques, and we wanted to see how her procedures could open up a thinking of the event. We were truly interested in how the force of language could be used as a technique for both thinking and making across our different vocabu-laries. And so, instead of debating, we found ourselves in an extremely generative dialogue, composing across modes of inquiry. This created, I think, the beginnings of an existential territory that is difficult to come by in academic circles, where opinions often hold more sway than procedural interventions capable of co-composing techniques and modes of speaking. Such an approach

[5] Madeline Gins and Arakawa, *The Architectural Body* (Tuscaloosa: University of Alabama Press, 2002).

takes time, it takes a willingness to risk one's ideas, a sense of openness, and it takes an event or project. This cannot be done in the abstract. In the case of coming together with Madeline Gins, it was done in the context of bringing our two worlds together through the 'Enter Bioscleave' event. The reason the event is key is that it is through the event that the techniques will be experimented with, and it is in the event that we will be able to see how our convergences of approach resonate. How the procedures unfold, what the techniques for relation do, will be key to seeing whether they are generative of emergent collectivity or whether they need to be tweaked towards future experimentation. And how they will be tweaked will then have an effect on how we determine the stakes of the event, which will of course be different for each of us. For Arakawa and Gins, the stakes are 'reversible destiny', which involves an account of immortality which we follow only to the extent that we are invested in emergent collectivities that go on living across their perishings, in lines of variation. Again the stakes connect but they are not the same. They don't connect in a commonality – they connect in the urgency of a procedural approach, in the urgency of a project.

Brian Massumi: What really interested me in that exchange, and what surprised me after four and a half hours of discussion about Arakawa and Gins's work and how it relates to the SenseLab's work, was when Madeline suddenly said, 'What are we going to name these procedures?' For her, we weren't just sharing ideas or communicating about ourselves and our past activities. A discussion is not just a discussion, for her. It's always doing something – or a something doing moving into a pragmatic unfolding at a later phase. What interested her was distilling pragmatic working points from the discussion, and then honing them as procedures that can be set in place in particular situations to condition events of emergence. Naming is a technique for fixing the procedures, in the sense that you fix a compound. It gives you a practical handle on what region of potential you've collectively brought to provisional expression, and holds it together in a way that you can do things with. This is a very different use of language than the way academics usually communicate. When you go to a conference, you can't help being subjectively positioned, from the moment you put on your name badge. You are not just registering your presence, you're representing yourself, and you speak accordingly. Your angle of entry into the situation is personalized in this way.

This assumes that your identity coincides with your potential, and that when we express ourselves, it's in this individualized mode of potential. It is exactly doing what Simondon warns against: mistaking the field potential from which an individuation emerges for the interiority of a subject. Needless to say, it creates anxiety. It cuts off many other modes of activity and catalysings of relation that could make the situation more of an event, and more open-ended. The question the SenseLab started with was, how do we make ourselves an event? How do we come together actively, as artists, academics and activists, in ways that don't just reproduce the usual genres of 'communication'? What relational procedures, or techniques of relation, can we collectively invent, name and put into situational practice for making events that truly deserve to be called events?

We realized very quickly that the kind of techniques we were looking for had to be impersonal. By that we meant directly collective, like Simondon's preindividual field in its transindividual becoming. That makes it sound a bit exalted. But it's really nuts and bolts, procedural in the best sense. The question is always 'how?' For example, how do you enter into a situation without just registering your representation of yourself? What conditions can be put in place to make that entry happen on another footing? How do you gesture to participants as they cross the threshold to the event that this time it is an invitation to experiment collectively and invent? How do you say, nonverbally, in the way the event is conditioned, don't bring your products – bring your process. Don't bring your thoughts you've already had and rehearse them to us as part of positioning yourself – bring everything else, your passions, your appetitions, your tools and abilities, your intensest procedures, and connect into the situation from that angle. Don't perform yourself – co-catalyse a collective event with us. What that's saying is that you are hereby relieved from the imperative to represent yourself and to be judged accordingly. You can compose, using many more dimensions of what it is you bring into the situation than are normally activatable, in a conference for example. The measure of success of your contributions will not be whether they were correct, or complete, or even authentically you, but rather what affective force they brought to the event. That means that no contribution can be owned, because it doesn't have effectiveness in itself, but only as creating the conditions for yourself *and* others – as a gift of process potential or a catalyst that can only be effective in the way it resonates with others. When others take up your gift of potential, they take it places you couldn't have taken it by yourself – which then enables you to go places you couldn't have gone alone. When an event of this kind is working, a dancer might move into a philosophical text in a way they never thought they had the preparation to do. And a philosopher might find themselves translating concepts into movements. When things like that happen, it deserves to be called an event. Events are always transindividual, bringing out potentials that could never have been arrived at individually.

The use of language in this kind of situation is very different. On the one hand, it is procedural in Arakawa and Gins's sense. It is used to embed certain set of potentials in the situation in an open-ended way that can only be brought to expression collectively. On the other hand, the use of language is necessarily evocative, because what will transpire has not been predetermined, but has to eventuate, and how it eventuates is up for relational grabs, and will only be clear as the event unfolds. This evocativeness of potentials as yet not fully formed gives the procedural language a poetic edge. You can see this poetico-procedural use of language in Arakawa and Gins's writing. You can read it as poetry, and you can use it as an instructional manual for experiential event-making.

Erin Manning: Perhaps the form of language we resist the most is debate and general positioning without enacting concepts or bringing them into play. This is why we work so closely with philosophical texts in the process of event-planning. Our hope is to get away from general statements such as 'of course, as everyone knows...' and speak instead in ways singularly connected to the work we are engaged with. In the five hours we spent with Madeline that day, all of that time was used to engage with language at the level of the work we have to do and not at the level of positioning ourselves or of debate.

Brian Massumi: What bothers me about the question of debate is that it presupposes that the stakes are given, and with them opposing positions, so that the only question is who is going to represent which positions and how convincingly. What we are talking about is reinventing the stakes.

Christoph Brunner: Avoiding these kinds of pre-defined stakes and constantly re-enliving collective thinking, practising and writing, leads to a very different sense of necessity. The question of necessity then has to do with how to avoid generalizing the use of language, and how we think and talk about language. So it doesn't come as something which can be imposed in an academic way of naming. I am thinking here about Deleuze's work and how he writes against naming in the way it is usually practised because it imposes a prefigured structure that is not led by necessity in the immediacy of what you are relationally negotiating. What would be the politics of necessity in the way we're talking about it?

Erin Manning: Deleuze takes up the concept of necessity from Nietzsche. Nietzsche places the question of necessity in the event's asking – this comes across very clearly in the passage in *Thus Spoke Zarathustra* called 'Moment' – 'what is the mode of existence created in

the necessity of this particular decision?' What he means
by decision in this context is also a kind of Whiteheadian notion of decision, understood as the cut propelling
the continuing of a process, similar to the concept of
transduction in Simondon. It is not individual will. It
isn't about my going into this way of living because I
judge it necessary for me but rather, as you said, how
the event constructs its own forms of necessity. This
means that at many stages in our practices and processes
we are faced with having to re-conceive how we might
encounter necessity. Sometimes the necessity is really
frustrating. It doesn't appear as we wished or imagined
it would appear. This kind of approach to necessity
demands an incredible flexibility and real rigour in the
techniques and enabling constraints put into place and
what effects they produce. It demands a return to the
question of what the stakes are. How are they generated? What kinds of skills are available? How does this
particular act co-compose with other acts in the making?
All of those questions bear their own processes of necessity. We see our work as composing procedurally and
technically with those necessities in a way that produces
modes of existence we can live with.

Brian Massumi: We talk a lot about what we do as a
form of aesthetic politics. We think of it as aesthetic in
an extended sense of that word, as referring to the
'process of experience'. What the SenseLab does is
experiment collectively with the process of experience
as a practice of the event. When we say the word 'aesthetic' and put it together with politics a lot of the
people bristle because they think of the aesthetic as sort
of a realm of free play of unconstrained expression. For

us, on the contrary, the aesthetic is immediately in connection with necessities of life. There have to be stakes
for any activity to be compelling. The reason why a lot
of people are drawn to the kinds of events the SenseLab
organizes is that they feel they are beaten down in the
situations they live in every day in their home contexts
and institutions. It is not that there is no freedom in
institutional contexts, but the options for resistance are
pre-formatted by the modes of conformity that come to
dominate the situation. There is little room for invention. People come to our events out of a sense of necessity, as an issue of survival. Many feel held back or
battered down, and can't see how to keep going. They
may feel chronically fatigued, or that their creative
potential is being drained. Their powers of resistance
have been taxed too many times, and they're looking
for some way to recharge. It's not an escape into an
aesthetic field of free choice and unfettered expression.
It's a life necessity. What we provide in response to these
yearnings isn't an unconstrained environment. We often
repeat: if anything goes, nothing will come. What we
do is set in place, poetico-procedurally, enabling constraints. These are mechanisms designed to set certain
conditions in place allowing for an inventive interaction
to occur that is something like a structured improvisation. The situation is positively constrained: conditioned
in a way that we hope will create the conditions for a
process of collective expression to unfold, in the course
of which something unexpected might emerge. The
hope is that what does emerge might feed forward into
further experimentation, beyond this event's perishing,
in a kind of contagion of collective potential. For us the
aesthetic is not an escape from life. Quite the opposite:

it is a different way of engaging with the necessities of life. It is the element of necessity, and the collectivity of the process from the very start to beyond its perishing, that make this kind of experimentation with expressive potential political. It's a practice of a 'politics to come', to paraphrase the term of Deleuze's we talked about earlier.

6

What a body can do

Arno Boehler*: Spinoza's question 'Do we know what a body can do?' became a major research issue in your workshop with Erin Manning at Tanzquartier Vienna yesterday. What is the particular relevance of this question for your philosophical work and the work you do at the SenseLab?

Brian Massumi: This question is of great interest to me. I approach it from the point of view of process philosophy, which is centrally concerned with creativity, with where it is found in the world and how it expresses itself. The short answer to that famous question of Spinoza's, 'Do we know what a body can do?' is simply: 'No!' There are powers of improvisation, powers of invention in a body that we have only begun to plumb. There are bodily capacities that do not require the

---

* Interview by Arno Boehler (2013)

---

presence of a brain or, in animals with a brain, that function independently of conscious calculation. These include capacities that we would have to categorize as capacities to think. I have been writing recently about animality and instinct for a book called *What Animals Teach us about Politics*.[1] I have been particularly taken with the insistence of certain scientists and theoreticians that there is improvisation and even problem-solving in animals without brains.

Darwin himself is one of the famous cases. He spent many years observing earthworms in his back garden. He talks about the improvisational prowess of earth-worms in relation to how they perform basic functions like the necessity to close the holes of their burrows to keep invaders or moisture out. He says that there is a general schema to their actions, but that each earth-worm, in spite of being brainless, is capable of improvis-ing new solutions that take the contingencies of each situation into account. In other words, they *invent* vari-ations on the theme. He says explicitly that this attests to a kind of 'mental power' or degree of mentality in worms.

This for me is one of the interesting aspects of the question of what a body can do: 'Can a body think?' If you define mentality as Whitehead does – as the capac-ity to exceed what is given and to bring forth a novelty – then an improvisational variation playing on an instinctive activity, even in an animal without a brain, shows a certain degree or mode of mentality. This conception of mentality breaks down the Cartesian

[1] Brian Massumi, *What Animals Teach Us about Politics* (Durham, NC: Duke University Press, 2014).

distinction between the mental and the physical, but without simply collapsing them into each other, or bracketing one out. It forces you to rethink how you define the physical and the mental, how you parse them together.

For Whitehead, the physical dimension of the body corresponds to actions performed in conformity to the past, continuing along the same lines as it, following the same schema. Thus the physical is a principle of conformity to already-emerged form. What characterizes mentality is the capacity to go beyond that givenness to improvise new forms. Note that I said 'mentality', and not 'the mind'. Here, mentality is a mode of activity, and it functions not in opposition to the physical but with it and through it, by prolonging and renewing it.

Every instinctive action performed by animals – and what action could be said not to have an instinctive basis? – has to have both of these elements, the mental and the physical. It has to work them together, otherwise the animal's actions will be completely maladaptive. If an instinct were incapable of creating variations on its own theme, of inventing new flourishes, new forms for its own operation, then it could do little more than respond to the environment in a stereotyped way. This would be fine if the environment did not change. But the environment is always changing. So the animal's instinctive activity has to wrap itself around changes in the environment. It has to change apace with the changes. That could be defined as a first degree of creative mentality, occurring at the level of a body as a pre-reflexive operation, prior to and independent of self-reflective consciousness.

Arno Boehler: Nietzsche presented so many animals in his *Zarathustra*, probably to demonstrate the fact that there exists a pre-reflexive form of *life* even in our human, all too human mentality? Not as something external to human beings, but as a pre-human form of life *within* human beings that shows almost over-human capacities sometimes?

Brian Massumi: Nietzsche saw the 'over-human' as the re-assumption by the human of the animality of the human. So yes, he is very much thinking in the way you are suggesting.

When I was talking about instincts I was talking about something called the 'supernormal stimulus', which I prefer to call 'supernormal tendency'. It came out of early studies of instinct in ethology by Niko Tinbergen. An instinct was thought to be an automatic, machine-like triggering of a stereotyped sequence of actions by a particular stimulus. Tinbergen wanted to know exactly what the stimulus was for particular instinctive behaviours. He tried to isolate the perceptual factors that served as the trigger. He was assuming that there would be a fixed form or gestalt configuration that could be isolated as the stimulus. To his own surprise, he found that it was impossible to isolate a perceptual form that played that role. What he found was that the response was to relations – to a set of linked factors that couldn't be isolated out, and wasn't limited a priori to any particular perceptual qualities. He concluded that the stimulus was irreducibly *relational*, and that these relational stimuli did not work according to any principle of resemblance. He was led to that conclusion by trying to make decoys that resembled the forms that the animals normally encountered in nature, then varying the characteristics of the decoys to see what factors were necessary to prompt a response. He found that there were no elements that could not vary, and that the most 'natural' forms actually prompted less 'passionate' results from the animals. Tinbergen himself speaks in terms of the passionateness of the responses. The most passionate responses were to deformations affecting more than one perceptual factor at the same time – in other words to changes in the *relational field* of experience. Not all relational-field deformations were equally impassioning. The ones the animals reacted to the most strongly were ones that *intensified* the perceptual qualities of the field – for example by heightening contrast. Even after figuring that out, Tinbergen still couldn't predict the response. It was being improvised. It was in some way spontaneous. Tinbergen did not really know what to do with that, because it didn't fit his theoretical framework. He just threw up his hands and said, it's forever a mystery. But we can draw the conclusion that there is a tendency towards deformation that runs in the direction of increased experiential intensity. This tendency is inherent to instinct itself, so that it is in the nature of instinct to create variations on its own operation, from a spontaneity of experience. Instinct is creative by nature.

What Tinbergen found, even though he didn't want to acknowledge it, was that at the heart of instinct there is a force of invention. This means that creativity is innate. It is in our nature. You could even say that we are most in touch with our animality, with what is most singular in animal life, when we surpass the given in a creative way. This fundamentally calls into question the tendency of theorists to define animal life in terms of adaptation, as neo-Darwinians do. In fact, it calls all normative thinking into question, suggesting a need to think much more about the *super*normal – about what creatively exceeds the typical and refuses to be limited by resemblance to past forms.

As I mentioned earlier, Whitehead defines the conformity or conformation between past events and present events as the physical pole of nature. You have to think in terms of the co-functioning, or co-operation, of two tendencies. On the one hand, you have a tendency of the present to extend into the future in conformity with what happened in the past. This is a tendency towards homeostasis, towards a discharge of intensity or a return to equilibrium. On the other hand, you have an equally strong tendency towards the supernormal, towards intensive deformation exceeding the givenness of instinctive schemas and their adaptation to the environment – towards the invention of forms. This is the aspect of activity that Whitehead defines as mental.

The important point for me is that you cannot think the two tendencies separately. It is not an alternative. The mental and the physical are not opposites, they are co-operants. They are two dimensions of the same operation. Two poles of *activity*. Their co-operation is eventful. It comes in episodes.

It makes no sense to define mentality or the physical outside of events. They have to be thought of as contrasting dimensions or modes of activity that co-occur within every event. If you look at it that way, it's no longer a question of *the* mind or *the* subject. You can't contain the activity of mentality in a noun. Nor can you talk about the body as a substantial thing. You can't reduce it to substance. You are talking about a mental pole and a physical pole; a mental dimension and a physical dimension; a tendency towards abstraction or extraction from the given, and a tendency towards the stability to be had by prolonging forms of givenness. When you get rid of the substantives, what you are left with are adverbs – qualities of events.

If you say, 'Isn't life the answer?' to the question what a body can do, the answer is 'Yes'. But you have to make life an adverb: lively. It's about liveliness or liveness. There is no life substance. Life is not a thing. Life is the way in which the mental and physical poles of events come together – differently every time, always under singular circumstances, moving in the general direction of the accumulation in the world of differences, of improvised novelty. Whitehead says that life is in the intervals between things – in the way things relate, in the way they come together in events under the dominant tendency towards the generation of new forms, or ontogenesis.

The tendency towards ontogenesis cannot operate without the contrasting tendency towards homeostasis. Life can't always live at the limit. It can't continue to survive if it is always pushing to the limit of intensity, creating new forms. It needs a degree of stability, oases of rest. It cannot be chaotically far-from-equilibrium at all times. It has to find its footing, to brace itself for new becomings. This means that life is the movement between the mental and physical poles, between conformation and supernormal excess, between one event and another, between all of the various factors in play. Life lives in the gaps. Still, what I just called the supernormal tendency, corresponding to the mental pole, is the dominant tendency. Life is biased in its direction – otherwise it would not be so changeable. We wouldn't have the exuberant proliferation of forms that we see in nature and in culture.

Arno Boehler: In the workshop you uttered the claim that contemporary philosophers have to construct a relational form of logic to think this 'liveliness' and thereby deconstruct the classical binary form of logic?

Brian Massumi: To stay for a moment with the question of life, I would say that a life is not an in-itself, it's an outdoing-itself. In other words, it follows a tendency to exceed already-realized potential in an actualization of new potential. That process, as you said, is relational. In order to think relation as primary, we need a different kind of logic, because the traditional logic is one of separation. Traditionally, the basic logical gesture is to separate X from not-X, and then define the common characteristics justifying inclusion of a given case in the set of X's. It starts with exclusion and ends in sameness. That doesn't get you to a process of outdoing-itself. It gets you to a stable structure of thought that cannot move. If you try to undo that logic, you have to accept that you cannot operate with the principle of the excluded middle – X or not-X. But you also have to go beyond deconstructing that exclusionary logic. You have to go on to affirm a more encompassing logic that is able to deal with what I call 'mutual inclusion'. When you get to that territory, you find that it's mined with paradoxes that you cannot avoid. You have to figure out how to make them productive. In that logic there are more terms than X and non-X, because of the included middle.

In my talk last night here at Tanzquartier Wien
I was talking about the virtual as a kind of emergence.
I talked about a very simple optical illusion called
the Kanizsa triangle, where there are three corners
that are black circles, but there is an angle cut out of
each, so that together they suggest the corners of a
triangle. You see a triangle, even though the lines of
the triangle are not actually there. I was talking about
how the disjunctive plurality of discrete elements
that are separated from each other with no actual connection between them creates the conditions for an
appearance that I call a pop-out effect. This is an emergence effect. It comes unrefusably, proposing itself to
vision. It's an immediate, unrefusable vision of something which is not actually there, but which defines
what the situation is all about for our perception. It
makes the situation be about how we cannot not see
what isn't actually there – a real, virtual triangle, or
what I call a 'semblance' in *Semblance and Event*. The
triangle is virtual in the sense that there are no actual
lines connecting the corners. It is virtual, and yet it
appears. The triangle, although virtual, is real, if by
real we mean what has the power to insist on its
own presence, which we have to accept regardless: we
cannot not see it. The reality of this virtual triangle
makes the situation about how the invisible, or more
generally the imperceptible, may come to characterize
an event. Even though this effect is predictable and
repeats, given the condition, there is still a newness to
it, because that emergence of the shimmering triangle
that we see without seeing it is in a way fresh every
time. There is something surprising about its insistence
on appearing.

The Kanisza Triangle

The point of the talk yesterday was that you cannot separate out the logic of pluralities from the logic of unities, because unities are emergent from pluralities. They supervene as events of relation occurring *across* the separation between the givenness of diverse elements. Something happens *between* the circles with the angles cut out. The triangle emerges to fill the distance between them. It appears as an expression of their separation, as well as an expression of its own virtual reality as the figure we see without actually seeing – as its own unitary, non-decomposable, immediate and unrefusable pop-out effect.[2]

I was trying to say that there are two logics happening at the same time. The two always co-occur, but you can attend to one at the expense of the other. For example,

[2] For an extended analysis of this example extending towards a theory of value, see Brian Massumi, 'Envisioning the Virtual', in *The Oxford Handbook of Virtuality*, ed. Mark Grimshaw (Oxford: Oxford University Press, 2014), pp. 55–70.

you can count the sides of the virtual triangle. But while you're doing that, you are not experiencing the immediacy of the pop-out effect. You're not attending to the surprise of the emergence of a triangle that you cannot not see even though it isn't there. There is a mutual implication – a co-implication – of the diverse and the unitary as aspects of the same event. In order to account for the event, you have to use a kind of logic that is about how different aspects co-compose, how they are mutually included in the same event. You miss the event if you put the unitary and the diverse, the emergent and the given, into opposition to each other. The pop-out triangle is the occurrent unity *of* that diversity. It would not be there without that diversity. The diversity conditions the appearance of the triangle, but that emergence is not reducible to them.

This is a very simple example that is in some ways very limited. You might still be tempted to think about it in terms of an opposition between the physical and the mental. For example, you could make a dichotomy between the material conditions – the ink on the page or pixels on the screen – and the subjective effect. But even in this simple example, it is more complicated than that, because the conditions of the triangle's emergence extend to other factors enveloped in the sensuous form of the corners: our body's tendency to fill in the gaps, and in particular its arguably innate orientation towards Platonic forms like the triangle. The materiality of the corners would be nothing, for the event of the triangle, without this non-sensuous contribution of tendency – which comes to expression in the form of the non-sensuous triangle. The triangle is also non-sensuous because its lines do not correspond per se to any sense input. What we often like to separate out as physical as opposed to mental or subjective always criss-cross, they always envelop each other – they are always complexly mutually including.

When I was talking about going beyond the logic of the excluded middle towards a logic of mutual inclusion, I was referring to this intertwinement: the included middle, the criss-crossing between mentality and physicality that is a requisite factor in the ontogenesis of live effects.

The logic of this mutual inclusion is neither the logic of the disjunctive plurality, nor the logic of the dynamic unity that is its virtual expression. It's the logic of their inter-involvement. It has to do with what Bergson calls pure multiplicities, as different from plurality, or diversity in the sense of a set of countable elements. Bergson says that there are phenomena consisting in a continual turnover of qualitative changes that actively interpenetrate, that include each other in process. You can't separate them out, and you cannot count them, because there are zones of overlap, zones of indistinction where they are absorbed in each other, and because the turnover is so quick that there is never a moment where you could point to a separate figure as a unity, in the way the Kanizsa triangle stood out as a unitary figure.

He says that these qualitative multiplicities of change are tendencies, an idea I find extremely useful. He says that tendencies do not relate to each other in the way that objects relate to each other. Objects are rivals. They cannot be in the same place, they mutually exclude each other. Tendencies, on the other hand, may clash, but even as they clash, they can participate in each other – as in the way we say that love and hate do. Tendencies can interpenetrate, without losing their own character. Each tendency is characterized by a certain mode or rhythm of unfolding. Bergson calls it a 'theme', as in music. His idea is that in the incipience of an experience, at that pre-reflective level, where thinking is just coming about, at a level which cannot be separated from the body, there is an activation of a multiplicity of tendencies in a state of mutual interpenetration. The mutual inclusion is of tendencies activating without yet unfolding. But they are all together in the activation, resonating and interfering with each other, agitating among themselves to come to expression. This is what I call bare activity. What ends up occurring is a resolution of this bare-active tension. A dominant tendency might end up expressing itself, or it's possible that a new tendency will emerge from the agitation. Even when a dominant tendency expresses, it will have been inflected in some way by its birth pains. It is only when the resolution comes that pluralities and unities appear. The tendential multiplicity expresses itself in a co-occurring of countable elements and pop-out unity effects. So you have a logic that has three levels, or dimensions: tendential multiplicity (qualitatively different modes of activity that you can't separate out temporally or spatially); plurality (the diversity of discrete, countable elements that are spatialized); and the unity *of* those elements (a virtual pop-out effect, which appears in space but without occupying it, and fills the moment with a timeless figure, in the case of the example I used, a Platonic form).

All three dimensions enter into every event. It is the last aspect, the reality of the virtual, that finally characterizes the event, that expresses what it will have all been about. It's the pop-out effect that says, to use the same example again, 'this is a triangular event'. When you move to more complicated events, you have to find correspondingly complex ways of talking about the untimeliness of the virtual realities that characterize events. Platonic forms are just the simplest, most limited case. Without going into details now, in my talk last night I introduced a renewed concept of 'value' to talk about this.

The logic of mutual inclusion I've been talking about is a logic of qualitative difference, taking modes of activity (tendencies) as its object, rather than either objects in the substantialist sense, or subjects in the sense of an agency you could separate out from the event's occurrence. As Nietzsche said, there is no doer separate from the deed. One of the aims of this logic is to take account of the quantitative, of the plurality of countable elements, but as part of a philosophy of qualitative becoming.

Arno Boehler: Which produces a big problem for measuring these kind of events, because you cannot reduce them to the counting system. It is not simply a problem of numbers.

Brian Massumi: It's fundamentally unmeasurable, even though there are measurable factors involved that are a necessary dimension of the event. Retrospectively, many of the contributing factors can be measured. But they are measurable only to the extent that they have become inactive, or can be treated as inactive, as traces of the event's passing. Like when I was talking about counting the sides of the triangle as killing the liveness of its event. While you're counting, you're no longer experiencing the aliveness, the surprise of the pop-out effect.

Arno Boehler: So we can only see it afterwards…

Brian Massumi: Yes. In the event, the countable diversity is already there, but it is there as a potential, because seeing a triangle implies the threeness of the sides. But we don't see it as a lateral threeness – we see it as the oneness of the triangle that takes the three sides up into its own unity. The diversity is enveloped in the unity of the emergent effect. That effect is not measurable as such. It is the *singularity* of the qualitative character of the event, more than it is a oneness of a triangle. What I mean is that the 'unity' of the triangle is different from the 'one' of counting. It's not a one after which a two will come. It's a one that finalizes everything that has entered into the event. That oneness that is the unity of that triangle has enveloped the plurality of the visible corners, as well as the multiplicity of the non-sensuous factors that enter in on the level of bare activity, in its own popping up.

So, in the end the unity of the triangle is supernumerary. It is beyond the logical measure of the event, because that triangle shouldn't actually be there – and actually isn't. It's extra, surplus. It's a surplus-value. The qualitative character of the event is what gives it its lived value, but the value is in the end a surplus-value. On the side of bare activity, the potentials mutually included as tendencies are also supernumerary, in the sense that you cannot divide them from each other and come up with a count, because in addition to each tendency there are the zones of indistinction between tendencies corresponding to their inter-involvement with each other, and there are also the transitions between tendencies turning over in agitation, not to mention any new tendencies that might be brewing in all that complexity. Count them as you wish, but there will always be more – a surplus or remainder. At either end, in the incipience of event and in its final characterization, there is a more-than – what Deleuze calls 'extra-being'. This gives a pronounced asymmetry to the world that keeps it lively. It keeps it off balance. The balance-sheet of becoming is always off kilter. The final tally is always an open question. Because of this, the world is always capable of surprising.

Arno Boehler: If we enter a room in a certain situation a pre-reflexive force of life is forcing us already to configurate the room in a certain way long before we have started to think in a self-reflexive manner. Could you say something about this force?

Brian Massumi: Last night I repeated what Bergson said about walking into a room for a lecture. That's a genre of activity he was very familiar with, of course. He knew the parameters, implicitly, without having to reflect on them. They were so thoroughly engrained in him as to operate pre-reflexively. Still, every time he opened the door to walk in to give a lecture, he was surprised. There was something different about the situation. Each time it had a singular feel about it, due to the mix of people, how they self-presented, the moods they happened to be in, maybe something about the time of day, or even the weather. Each time, he walked into a relational milieu that had its own unique complexion, a unique affective tonality, even though the kind of event that was about to take place was so well known to him. Crossing the threshold of any event, you move into a relational field that presents a certain newness, no matter how hackneyed the occasion. Almost all events do belong to a genre. It is of the nature of events to come in series. To the extent to which the event belongs to a series, it carries certain generic presuppositions that are immediately in play. They are like default settings that activate as we cross the threshold. But the event can never be reduced to its conformity to those default settings. Looked at from another perspective, the presuppositions in play are a necessary enablement for the difference in what happens – just as the structures of musical genres are a necessary enablement for improvisation. The variation on what happens can go so far as to make the genre itself cross a threshold, in which case a new genre might emerge, as was the case with jazz. When the variation stays within the perceived bounds of its received genre, it still enlivens. It gives the genre the power to remain compelling, even after so many repetitions, and to continue producing variations on itself as it continues its seriation.

The point about the newness and variation of even the most pre-formatted events is important because it relates the concept of presupposition – the notion that there are pre-reflexive default settings informing our activity that are activated at the threshold to events – to the multiplicities of potential I was just talking about in terms of tendency. The theory of presupposition that I find most useful comes from the pragmatic linguist Oswald Ducrot. He describes the presuppositional fields of language as the active involvement of nonverbal forces in the speech act. He gives a very simple example, of entering a field. You go in, without realizing that it's occupied. Suddenly, you find yourself face to face with a bull, staring at you from across the paddock. Ducrot says that the dawning realization upon crossing the threshold of the situation catalyses a field of potential. Before you have had time to think, you have already sized up the mood of the bull. Without actually going through the steps of a calculation, you have already assessed how far you are from the gate. You have noticed, not quite consciously, whether there is mud and whether the ground is slippery. You have hypothesized which direction the bull might come at you from, where you might run in response. A whole field of potential composed of lines of potential action, and their enabling or disenabling conditions, breaks into your life. It all happens in an instant, in an interval smaller than the smallest interval of conscious reflection. Retrospectively, you might describe the event in a way that implies that you arrived at an awareness of the characteristics of the situation by inductive observation, or that you deduced which course of action would be best. But you didn't actually perform these logical operations, with their separate steps. It all happened so quickly that there wasn't time for a logical operation. It all came at once, not as deduction, nor as an induction, but as what C.S. Peirce calls an 'abduction': a realization that comes flush with perception's dawning. This is not a logical operation, but a life operation. It is lived as a dimension of the live event. It was not you standing back and thinking about the event. It was the event thinking itself through you.

———————

What a body can do

So, every time you cross a threshold as you make your way through life, you are moving into one presuppositional field after another. Each is actually a co-involvement or co-implication of a set of potential qualitative changes – potential moves that alter the terrain of life. When you transition from one situation to another, what you move into is a mutual inclusion of alternative potentialities presenting themselves integrally, as a singular relational milieu. This happens before you know it – or as you know it, abductively. Active participation precedes conscious perception. It is you who are inducted into the situation, almost in the military sense, before you reflectively perform any inductions about it. You are drafted into the situation, and are already to some extent constrained by the lay of the participatory land in which you find yourself. You are constrained in the sense that the active potentials enveloped in the relational milieu are conditioned by the situation. But there are always degrees of freedom – precisely because what presents itself is a landscape of alternative potentials, and not a fait accompli. It's not over until it's over. There are any number of things that could happen, by your own actions, or the bull's, or by chance, that might modulate the field's complexion of potential, altering its presuppositions on the fly. Even a slight gesture, a most nuanced movement on your part, could change the posture of the bull towards you. You could do a number of things, but you don't have the time to step aside and consider the situation. You *act* the decision. Your enacting acts *as* a decision.

Even when a movement of yours modulates the field of potential, it is still the event that is thinking through you. You are acting in and on that thinking through. I talk about this in *The Power at the End of the Economy*. Decision is always a collaborative undertaking, between you and situational factors – including nonhuman ones like bulls and mud. The decision involves both poles, the mental and the physical, defined as we were talking about earlier. And by those definitions, the mentality and physicality involved do not parse out along the traditional lines. All the mentality is not in you. If mentality is the mode of activity whereby what eventuates surpasses the given, then the potentials in you*r encounter* with the field are 'mental'. The bull and the mud and the gate of the bull pen participate in the mentality of the situation as much as your subjective states do. William James succinctly expresses this distributive nature of mentality when he poses the question of consciousness by asking not 'what does it mean for me to be conscious *of* a pen?' but rather 'what is it to be conscious *in* a pen?' He was referring to his writing instrument, but in relation to this example it works just as well with the other definition of a pen.

Arno Boehler: Yesterday you ended your talk on the virtual with a high valuation of care as a virtue. Even the extra-being of virtue is not coming from outside a concrete situation, but rather immanently, from within its own virtual potential?

Brian Massumi: In my talk last night, I tried to develop Whitehead's idea that care or concern is a quality of the event, and can't be reduced to the interiority of a subject. If that is the case, then you would have to be able to find some modality or degree of concern in every event – even the event of the appearance of a triangle that isn't actually there. The three circles with angles cut out that the triangle takes for its corners are discrete elements. In themselves, they are a simple disjunct plurality of separate things. They don't concern each other. They don't relate to each other, other than by resemblance – which is something we as perceiving subjects add to their separateness, in an operation of judgement that comes from outside their plane. However, in the event, we and they are on the same plane – the plane of the event. We are absorbed in the appearance of the triangle, unitarily popping out from their diversity. When the triangle emerges in all immediacy, it brings to expression a relation that what are now its corners do not have in themselves, in their simple diversity. It is only as they come out of themselves into the appearance of the virtual triangle that they come to relate. This is not a function of their resemblance to each other, but of their *distance* from each other – the differential between them. The triangle seizes upon the differential, or 'prehends' it, to use Whitehead's vocabulary. It is this emergent prehension that makes them concern each other. They concern each other in the *event* of the triangle's *appearance*. The virtual triangle is the form in which their concern for each other actually appears. You could say that this is a certain mode or degree of care. And you could generalize that. Wherever there occurs a holding together of elements as they are taken up in the production of an effect that exceeds their simple plurality, there is an emergent relation that makes the separate elements immediately concern each other. This applies to any event, everywhere in the world, on any level of matter or of thought – and everywhere between. Care or concern is always a factor in the genesis of events, even aside from the issue of human perception – even in material events in the absence of a human perceiver. An atom 'prehends' the subatomic particles composing it. Its unitary form is the form of expression of their eventfully concerning each other. Whitehead goes so far as to say that concern is an 'ultimate factor' of the world. It is not a content of human subjectivity.

Arno Boehler: That sounds very Heideggerian!

Brian Massumi: Perhaps…I hope not. I'm not sure if Heidegger would take it as far into the nonhuman world and away from language as Whitehead would. In any case, going back to the recognizably human level, care is the way in which relational unities eventfully emerge that recursively give the diversity of contributing elements a concern for each other that they don't have in themselves – as well as obliging us to have a concern for that event. That obligation comes to us through the concern that the contributing elements have for each other. If the concern pre-exists, you are in a completely different ethical and political domain. You are in the domain of already constituted beings with established needs and preferences – the instrumental domain of interest and conscious calculation. Or, you're in the realm of a priori moral imperatives. In either case, the concern is something you project subjectively onto the event. It's not something that *occurs to you* – both in the sense of absorbing you in an event, and in the sense of an emergent realization. Whitehead's concept of concern is not subjective. It is in the terrain of ontogenesis, of the becoming that comes of the co-operation of mentality and physicality, as coincident poles of the event that cut across the subject–object divide, as I was saying before when I was talking about the distributed nature of mentality.

Now, instead of corners of a triangle, let's take the example of a group of people in a room at a political discussion. If you consider each person individually, you're in the domain of interest. Each person brings to the discussion their own already-arrived-at positions and priorities, and they represent those interests in the discussion. But that is not all they bring. They also bring their tendencies and desires – in a word, their potential to become. The potential of individuals to become does not necessarily coincide with their interests as already-constituted individuals. It does not necessarily coincide with their personal interests, as narrowly defined according to prevailing criteria of rationality or utility. Through the encounter with the group, something else might occur to them. Who they are as individuals might be modulated by emergent field potentials – angles of approach to the problem they would never have thought of individually, paths of action that hadn't presented themselves before. To the extent that these novelties appear as a function of the group dynamic, the individuals involved are coming out of themselves. They are coming out of their simple diversity as individuals, and coming into concern for each other, in an emergence that takes them all up together. Just as the triangle emerged from the differential between the diversity of what became its corners, this political coming-into-concern of separate individuals emerges from the differential between their respective tendencies and desires.

So, on the human level of politics and ethics, care has to do with the co-composition of potentials towards the emergence of an extra-being of the individuals involved – a more-than-individual expression of their coming-together to shape a relational milieu that belongs to them collectively. The 'more-than-individual' is a term from Gilbert Simondon. He calls the fields of potential we have been talking about 'transindividual'. From this perspective, politics is about the transindividual modulation of fields of relation rather than the representation of a subjective point of view or personal interests – or even group interests. Interest is just the wrong concept. It begins with what separates, and doesn't give the tools to get beyond that division. It's a concept that is divisive by nature, and we see the political consequences of that every day.

The concept of interest is predicated on a certain notion of value that reduces it to instrumental ends. Now we're ready to return to the question of value. The approach I've been describing suggests another concept of value. You can call a 'value' anything that characterizes a situation – anything that sums up the singular character of the event in which the constituent differentials, tensions and tendency of the situation culminate. The virtual triangle that is seen without actually being seen is a perceptual value summing up that episode of vision. In more complex situations, such as interactions between people in the political context, the value is the singular quality of aliveness, the mode of vitality expressing itself in that encounter as its vitality affect. That mode of vitality has value, or is a value, because it sums up a coming-together of tendencies in an emergent figure. The process of that coming-together towards that emergence will add itself to the world as another available tendency. Once a value, always a value, in potential. A value is not just reflective of the character of an event. It becomes a key factor in the generation of events that express potential, and that forward it on to subsequent events. A value, once emerged, remains as an attractor for other events to come. It is that forward-pulling attractive force towards the recurrence of a mode of coming-together-for-expression that defines an existential value.

An existential value is a surplus-value of life, in the sense that it carries a force of extra-being, of becoming. A surplus-value of life is always collective, but not in a sense of a simple aggregation of individuals as countable elements of a set. It is collective in that truly transindividual sense in which things come into supernumerary relation with each other through the potentials they activate, and surpass themselves in a joint movement constituting the dynamic unity of their differential. The collective is not just an aggregate of individuals. It is a co-individuation. For that reason, Simondon always uses the term collective individuation.

Arno Boehler: You seem to rethink the political from a perspective of highlighting the sharing of potentials of divergent fields, actualized in events. That means we have to give up the concept of self-centred points and replace them through the concept of transindividual fields of relations?

Brian Massumi: Yes. We participate jointly in life. We don't have to give up care for the self, however – only the self-centredness. We have to embed care for the self in relational becomings – for the existential empowerment of the self and the other. A collective individuation is a correlated becoming through which individuals receive a boost of extra-being from their participation in an event that surpasses them as individuals. For that, the concept of affect is much more fundamental than the concept of interest. The differentials, tensions and tendencies that go into making a collective individuation are capacities to affect and to be affected, which co-compose to form complex fields of reciprocal capacitation. Thinking affectively means thinking in terms of ecologies of potential and the events that express and vary them.

This changes the meaning of the word 'care'. What you're really caring for is not your separate self, or other individuals. You are caring for both through a care for the event, in the way that Erin Manning talks about it in her work. Care for the event is care for the relational field as such – care for what can come of the events brewing in the field in terms of what I talked about earlier as a supernormal intensification culminating in the creation of a qualitative surplus-value of life for all involved. Surplus-value of life is not given and it is not found. It is created. This creative aspect gives an aesthetic dimension to the political thinking of the care for the event. It also implies that there are techniques for modulating fields of relation – techniques of relation that have to be thought and practised differently from techniques of individual expression, or group techniques of the kind we normally refer to when we think of the political, such as debate and negotiation. The dominant techniques for political expression and negotiation of interests are techniques of interaction. Interaction, as I argued in *Semblance and Event*, is very different from relation. It is inter-individual, as opposed to

What a body can do

transindividual, and communicational as opposed to
ontogenetic. We need to hone our techniques of relation, and create cultures at the intersection of politics
and aesthetics that foster them.

   This has consequences for how we think about
freedom. It is through relation that we derive greater
potential, intensify our powers of existence. Freedom is
never individual. It is by nature relational.

Arno Boehler: So we are back to Spinoza and the creation of the body, which is some-body, who affects and
can be affected.

Brian Massumi: Exactly. A body*ing*.

In lieu of a conclusion

As announced in the preface, the aim of this book has not been to prescribe solutions but to pose better problems. A 'better' problem is one that provides a jumping-off point for others to continue from in their own way, along their own exploratory paths, for intensities of experience to come. A 'good' problem is one that wears its inconclusiveness like a badge of merit: a token of its problematic service of inviting and inciting. It is one that twists itself around its own loose ends to tie itself into an alluring knot, like a ribbon around a gift of process. The gifts of process I have received from the authors and interlocutors whose thinking infuses the preceding interviews have been more than alluring. They have been tools of life, and resources for survival. It is hoped that this book has been able to pay the favour forward, in however small a way.

There are a number of oft-repeated misconceptions about affect and its political implications which, if not borne in mind and held at bay, devalue the intended gift before it is taken out of the box. An attentive reader of the interviews will already recognize how off the mark these notions are. In lieu of a conclusion, here is a rundown of the most prominent of these missed conceptions:

Affect is individual. Affect is transindividual. It is ontogenetically prior to the distinction between the individual understood as separate unit and the collective understood as a molar aggregate of separate units. It is 'collective' in the sense that it expresses itself in collective individuations (emergent populations of individuals whose formation is processually correlated at a distance, across their differences).

Affect is asocial. Corollary: *Affect must be socialized through mechanisms of mediation.* Affect, as the openness to being affected, is directly relational. It is pure sociality, in the sense of the social in the openness of its incipiency, ready to become all manner of social forms and contents. That readiness is not simply a passive availability. It is an active pressure towards taking-form. It has an appetite for its own eventuation and final characterization. It is an as-yet indeterminate determination to be determined. It is tendency: a determination to be determined with an appetite not only to express itself, but to do so repeatedly, with something happening differently every time, at least in some small way. Far from being asocial, affect is the ongoing force of the social taking evolving form. Affect comes to determinate expression through actually occurring encounters. The evolving social expression of affect hinges on the immediacy of events. The events relay each other, forming event series, tracing lineages of recurrence. Tendencies are brought to serial expression in and through events. What recurs in each event in the lineage is the immediacy of this evolving taking-form. Affect is the ongoing immediation of the social.

Affect's social expression is in mass psychology. Mass psychology only understands the collective as a molar aggregate of individualities that have melted into an undifferentiated magma. This is understood to occur when the mediation of socializing mechanisms fails. This idea presupposes a notion of the individual body as the seat of biological impulses that are fundamentally irrational in nature, and must be curbed by culture, or sublimated. Affect calls this entire complex of ideas into question. As pure sociality, affect is by nature transindividual. 'Transindividual', however, is not synonymous with 'collective' in the mass psychology sense. To the contrary, it expresses itself in movements of correlated differentiation. In itself, it is hyper-differentiated: mutually including all manner of differentiations in potential. Finally, affect is not psychological. As transindividual, directly relational and immediately eventful, it overspills on all sides the interiority of the psychological subject. Psychology is a particular mode of expression of affect that individualizes it. Mass psychology is a logical consequence of this individualization: once an individual interiority is constructed, its affective overspilling of its assigned boundaries can only be understood as a de-differentiating melding. The excess of potential that immediates affect, that makes it the force of the social taking form, is mistaken for a magmatic lack of form.

In lieu of a conclusion

The 'autonomy of affect' refers to the separation of the individual from the social. The autonomy of affect refers to the process by which the excess of potential that presses for expression is remaindered after every determinate taking-form, returning to in-form a next expression. The autonomy is of this process. The autonomy of affect is of the turnover of potential on itself, towards the proliferation of ongoing variations on its expression of socially formative force.

Affect pertains to 'raw' experience. There is no raw experience. All experience is in-formed by prior takings-form. The manner in which prior takings-form in-form subsequent expressions is always inflected by how potential makes ingress into a situation, with what gradations. The arc of potential's entry into a situation and through it is always modulated on the fly, by very particular mechanisms. Prime among these mechanisms are the 'abductions' that texture the landscape of potential through which a coming event will wend its way, in the first flush of its incipiency. Abductions are 'lived hypotheses'. They are thought in the immediacy of their enactment. This means that they are felt as directly as they are thought. They are thinking-feelings of the import of the situation at hand, replete with competing tendencies and alternative paths. Their enactive nature qualifies them as gestures. Thinking-feelings are speculative gestures: they convoke potential and carry alternatives. As gestures, they do this with style. They do it with technique. There is no expression of affect without technique. It is the nature of affect to be already cultured with technique.

In lieu of a conclusion

Affect is natural as opposed to cultural. Affect is of the nature of culture. Culture is coextensive with nature. Nature, in the narrower sense of the formative activity of the world outside the human sphere, is always already 'technical'. Nature is a self-running autonomy of process replete with its own speculative gestures. What is the trajectory of a body, for example, if not an enactive speculation on future position?

Affect is anything goes. Affect is always conditioned. Its expression, as it comes to be enacted, is always selective. Every situation of encounter imposes constraints on the selection of potential that will eventuate. The expression of affect, far from being anything goes, is an expression of necessity. It is just that it is always also an expression of the necessity of invention: an ongoing validation of the rule of variation: that the world is restless at heart and never sits still. An inventive variation takes constraints as enabling. There would be no creativity of dance without the constraint of gravity. Affect assumes necessity, in the strong sense of taking it on. It takes it on in such a way as to extract from it a surplus-value of creativity.

Affect is feel-good. This idea is a misunderstanding of the Spinozan concept of 'joy' that is often used in affect theory. Joy in the Spinozan sense refers to the intensity of the affective encounter. The intensity of the encounter in turn refers to an augmentation in powers of existence – capacities to feel, act and perceive – that occurs through the encounter. Understood in this way, joy is not synonymous with positive emotion. It is not 'happy', and it does not connote the attainment of satisfaction. These 'hedonic' distinctions simply do not apply to affect. They apply to emotions: the psychological capture of affect for the interiority of a supposedly individual subject. Subjects feel good about themselves emotionally (or not), in the personal refuge of their putative interiority. Affect feels out the world. It is by nature open to adventure, and adventures always involve hardship. Joy in adventure cannot be had without affirming the hardship, in the strong sense of taking it on creatively.

Affect is good. Affect is ethically neutral, in the normal understanding of ethics. That is why it must have its own ethics. As such, affect is neither good nor bad by prevailing ethical criteria. The ethics of affect has no normative value. Affect concerns the revaluation of values. It acknowledges norms only to exceed them, in becoming (including the becoming of the system of norms). This revaluation is desired. Or it is not. Affect is not prescriptive. It is promissory. What it promises is intensity. It is neutral as well in relation to political criteria of judgement. Affect can be fascistic or progressive; reactionary or revolutionary. It all depends on the orientation of the transindividual desires speculatively gestured into motion. The evaluation of affect bears on these tendential orientations. That evaluation has no power of prescription. It is not a judgement that can justify an orientation. It is a diagnosis that maps the promise of an encounter. The diagnosis is an eventful dimension of the speculative gesture. It is included in the enactment. The ethics of affect is therefore experimental. It operates on the level of enactive technique, and like all technique is honed through trial and error. Given the transindividual nature of affect, the techniques must be effectively, if speculatively, collective.

Affect pertains to the body as opposed to the psychic or mental. This is a misunderstanding that often arises from the distinction between affect and emotion. If emotion is the capture of affect in the interiority of a subject, then, the reasoning goes, affect must be objective in contrast to the subjectivity of emotion. The attention that affect theory has rightly given to neurophysiological phenomena, particularly those attesting to nonconscious dimensions of experience, has reinforced this false opposition by seeming to indicate that affect pertains to the physical functions of the organ of the body that is the brain. Affect does pertain to the body, but the body figures here in an extended sense. The body of affect is extended first in the sense that it is not limited to the brain. It extends throughout the body through the innervations of the flesh. It encompasses the nonconscious 'body knowledge' of habits, reflexes, the proprioceptive system, the many functionings of the autonomic nervous system, including the enteric nervous system or 'gut brain', and the myriad of sub-threshold experiences, or microperceptions, populating the body's every move. These form feedback loops that continually inflect overall experience without themselves rising to consciousness. They in-form thinking-feeling. The body of affect is extended in a more radical sense as well: it includes modes of activity normally designated as belonging to the mind. A habit, for example, is a power to generalize (to produce an operative resemblance between different events, which are always in some way singular). And from the complexity of the feedback between nonconscious and conscious dimensions of experience, new tendencies arise. These constitute enactive speculations on the future potential of activity. Affect theory does not reduce the mind to the body in the narrow, physical sense. It asserts that bodies think as they feel, on a level with their movements. This takes thinking out of the interiority of a psychological subject and puts it directly in the world: in the co-motion of relational encounter. If the Humean definition of the mental is accepted – as that which exceeds the given – then every bodily event is flush with mentality. Every act has a degree of mentality proportionate to its capacity to surprise. That capacity varies across the nature–culture continuum, but is never entirely absent, even in the supposedly mechanical workings of 'dumb' matter (as deterministic chaos theory has amply demonstrated). Affect requires a far-reaching re-evaluation of what a body can do. What is normally called the 'mind' is a reduction of the body's capacities to the sphere of reflective consciousness (which, as neuropsychology has amply demonstrated, is always accompanied by incipient, sub-threshold actions 'mirroring' what is being thought; this was known in process philosophy and affect theory long before the discovery of mirror neurons, under such names as 're-enaction', 'incipient action' and 'reactivation'). Concepts like 'thinking-feeling', 'non-sensuous perception', 'nonconscious experience' and 'bare activity' are designed to deal with the complexity of the body in this processually extended sense. They are ways of articulating how the body always includes the abstract (that which exceeds the given) in its own self-extending definition. Far from suggesting a physicalist reductionism, affect asserts that there is an expansive mental aspect, or what Whitehead calls a 'mental pole', to every bodily event.

Affect is prelinguistic. Every act of language involves an expression of affect. Affect is the infra-conditioning of every determinate activity, including that of language. The preferred prefix for affect is 'infra-'. 'Pre-' connotes time sequence. But affect always accompanies, on the parallel track of potential. 'Intra-' is also imprecise, connoting as it does space and containment (from *interus*, internal). 'Infra-' on the other hand connotes what actively lies below a certain threshold of appearance on an open-ended spectrum (as in 'infrared'; from *inferus*, below). The threshold of appearance designates a turning point where the spectrum changes qualitatively in nature, while retaining the continuity of its constitutive gradations (as when infrared shades into the visible region of the spectrum, which is also the qualitative turning point where heat becomes light). There is no antinomy between affect and language. There is accompaniment and becoming, always involving the full spectrum of the graded continuum of experience. The nonverbal grades on the continuum of experience are not in opposition to the verbal registers, any more than infrared is opposed to red. They companion them (as any infrared camera will show). The infra-linguistic registers of experience accompany linguistic expression. At the same time (and this is where the infrared analogy breaks down), they are in-formed by past linguistic expressions, through the complex feedback loops between nonconscious and conscious levels already described. And they in turn in-form linguistic expression with abductive thinking-feelings of the potential towards which speech acts may speculatively gesture, in their powerfully abstract way. The infra-linguistic register of experience in-forms language's capacity to modulate the mental pole of events. It primes and stokes language's singular ability to exceed the given (its power to fabulate). As with all of the dichotomies that figure in this list of missed affective conceptions, the relation between language and the nonlinguistic must be understood in terms of a graded continuum of potentials punctuated by thresholds past which the mode of activity expressing itself changes qualitatively in nature. Rather than oppositions, affect works with qualitative differentials: the integral mutual inclusion of qualitatively different potentials for expression on the same spectrum. It is always a question of degree. A pre-verbal human is already infra-linguistic. As is a nonhuman animal, to the degree to which it tends to express the mental pole of activity which language carries to its highest power.[1]

Affect negates freedom. This is the unjustified conclusion some commentators have drawn from discussions in affect theory of the famous 'missing half-second'. This refers to neurophysiologist Benjamen Libet's discovery that there is up to a half-second lag in the

---

[1] I argue in *What Animals Teach Us about Politics* that there is a mentality in all animal activity, attested to in even the most 'lowly' instinctive actions.

conscious dawning of an action from the onset of its physiological stirrings. In the lag, the coming action is moving from its own 'readiness potential' to its actual expression: from its in-acting as potential to its acting-out in gesture. What has bothered many people is that the transition is always already on its way nonconsciously, which is taken to mean that it negates freedom of decision. The idea that this non-conscious incipiency of action contradicts freedom must be revised in the light of what was said earlier about the mutual inclusion of mental and physical movements in every act's emergence. The erroneous idea that affect negates freedom results from a refusal to fundamentally rethink the body/mind duality: it construes the nonconscious activity of the body as purely 'physical' or 'physiological' as opposed to 'mental', and equates the physical with 'unthinking' mechanism. Affect theory, quite to the contrary, pre-supposes the mutual inclusion in every event of a physical pole (defined as the tendency of an event to conform to the ordering it inherits from the immedi-ate past) and a mental pole (defined as the tendency to surpass the given, to produce the new and generate surprise). Affect in no way excludes freedom. It does, however, require it to be redefined. The redefinition is necessary because the workings of affect do con-tradict freedom, if freedom in any way implies the body/mind, physical/mental duality. These dualities are so entrenched in conceptions of freedom that it is difficult for many to bend their thinking-feeling past them. Received ideas about freedom style it as the mental act of an individual psychological subject, or as an unconditioned decisional act of an individual

will. This divorces it from the body. But there is no
unconditioned decision. And there is no individual,
outside its own transindividual becoming, which
takes effect through affect (not in reflection). The
notion of individual will is sterile: it posits a vacuum
of subjective reflection in which volition functions in
glorious isolation, unconstrained and unconditioned.
This is not freedom. This is a fiction. The nature–
culture continuum abhors a vacuum. Freedom is not
a property of a subject. There is no pure capacity of
decision unmarked by necessity. Freedom is an
achievement, attained of necessity. It is not exercised,
it is invented, through the enabling modulation of
constraints. Its invention is situational. Situations are
eventful. And events are relational. Subjects don't
decide in a vacuum. Events decide, in relation.
Freedom pertains not to the individual, but to process.
Freedom is the transindividual autonomy of the affective process to generate surprises. It is not without
physicality – but it constitutes a triumph of mentality
(once again by its affective-processual definition as
the capacity to surpass the given and generate the
new). Do not protest your freedom. Enact surprise.
Speculate that.

Freedom

Index

abduction, 9–10, 15, 43–4, 94, 194–5, 207, 213; politics and, 18
abstract, 183, 212
academics, 71–4, 166–8, 170, 173
activist philosophy, 154
activity, 153, 182, 190, 193; affect and, ix, 7, 91, 150–2, 212; background, 155–6; consciousness and, 214; event and, 151; feeling and, 48; life and, 153; lived, 55; mentality and, 179, 196; potential and, 170, 211; thinking and, 106. *See also* bare activity; in-act
aesthetics, 106, 152; life and, 70, 175–6; politics and, 36, 66–8, 70, 100, 174, 202–3
affect, x–xi; activity and, 91, 150–2; appetition and, 205; becoming and, 209, 212; body and, 3–5, 7–9, 10, 12, 48, 50–2, 56–7, 92, 148, 210–15; capitalism and, 20–5, 30, 83, 89, 91, 111; difference and, 56, 63; ecology of, 122, 202; emotion and, 3–5, 31, 208–10; encounter and, 208; ethics and, 11, 34, 36, 209; event and, 47, 63, 91–3, 96, 115, 205–6; experience and, 1, 8, 51, 147–8, 207; expression and, 8, 11, 31–2, 205–8, 212–14; fascism and, 209; field and, 124, 148; force and, 92, 168, 205, 207; freedom and, 100, 213–15; ideology and, 85–7; intensity and, 3–7, 70, 208–9; language and, 7, 32, 44, 150–1, 212–13; misconceptions about, 204–15; modulation and, 31–2, 34, 55, 95–6; potential and, 5, 7, 11, 31, 36, 206–8, 211–13; power and, 19, 32, 34–6, 39, 48, 63, 86,

216

Index

112–13; relation and, ix–x, 17, 205–6; Spinoza on, ix, 3–4, 6, 48, 51, 91, 93, 97, 150, 177, 203; subject and, 4, 48, 150–1, 210–11; thinking-feeling and, 94, 96–7; transindividual and, 94–5, 98, 128, 205–6, 209–10; vitality, 141, 200. *See also* feeling; intensity; joy; microperception

affective attunement, x, 56, 68, 98, 101–2, 104, 121, 135, 141. *See also* affect; attunement

affective tonality, 61, 130, 193

affective politics, vii–ix, 18, 35, 56–8, 65–6, 68–70, 81, 100, 117–18, 123, 133, 139, 143, 146, 204. *See also* affect; politics

affective turn, 56, 122, 150

animality, 178–82, 213

anti-globalization. *See* globalization, anti-

anxiety, 159–67, 170

appetition, 153, 155, 171; affect and, 205

art, 71–4, 78, 80, 157

Artaud, Antonin, 44–5

attractor, 60, 62, 74; value and, 201

attunement: 57–8, 106, 133–134, 136; contrast and, 105; differential, 94–5, 98, 100, 115, 117, 119, 121, 131, 141, 148. *See also* affective attunement

autism, 125–9

autonomy, 37–9, 42; connection and, 40–1

bare activity, x, 52, 101–2, 105–6, 108, 110, 141, 143, 151–2, 189, 191, 211. *See also* activity

becoming, 12, 40, 42, 44–6, 48, 51–2, 71, 94–5, 98, 124, 144, 149, 154, 161, 183, 190, 192, 198, 201; affect and, 209, 212; ontopower and, 111, 116; transindividual and, 171, 215

belonging, 18, 41, 43; experience and, 45

Benjamin, Walter, 113, 128

Berardi, Franco 'Bifo', 152, 161

Bergson, Henri, viii, 6, 59, 119, 188–9, 192

biogram, 113, 117–18, 121–2, 133, 143. *See also* diagram

biopower, 108–11. *See also* ontopower; power

body, 13–14, 20, 49, 55, 104–5, 106, 177; affect and, 3–5, 7–9, 10, 12, 48, 50–2, 56–7, 92, 148, 210–15; capitalism and, 109–10; differential attunement and, 94–5; habit and, 64; individual and, 206; mentality and, 179; microperception and, 54; movement and, 141; potential and, 44–5, 68; relations and, 51; thinking-feeling and, 98, 101; thought and, 154, 178

bodying, 125, 144, 203

Bourdieu, Pierre, 85

Bush, George W., 32, 35, 57

Butler, Judith, 152

Index

and, 56, 63; attunement and,
94–5, 98, 100, 115, 117,
119, 121, 131, 141, 148;
body and, 54, 68, 98;
capitalism and, 89; face and,
92; habit and, 64; individual
and, 199, 205; repetition
and, 65, 103
disciplinarity, vii, ix, 77
disciplinary power, 20, 21,
28–30
Ducrot, Oswald, 193–4
duration, 61–3, 67, 129. *See
also* present, specious; time

ecology, 123, 127, 137, 149,
152; of affect, 122, 202;
capitalism and, 139;
emergence and, 136; event
and, 125–6, 168; life and,
117; media, 114; political,
18–19, 21, 113; of potential,
202; of practices, 42, 68, 70,
136, 140, 153, 166; of time,
129
economy, 1, 21, 27–8, 32, 38,
41, 79, 131, 133; qualitative,
137–9. *See also* capitalism;
gift; surplus-value; value
embodiment, 51, 70, 85, 120,
135; freedom, 98; process
and, 87–8. *See also* body
emergence, 18, 40, 71, 79, 87,
101–2, 105, 151, 155, 175,
197, 199–200, 214;
capitalism and, 109; ecology
and, 136; event and, 170,
191; experience and, 122,
129; field and, 103, 127,
149; micropolitics and, 81;
subject and, 52; thought and,
116; virtual and, 185–7

emotion, 7, 54, 141; affect and,
3–5, 31, 208–10
empiricism, radical, 123
encounter, 92–3, 96–7, 126;
affect and, 208; body and,
95; potential and, 196
environment, 79, 149, 154,
182; affect and, 57; change
and, 179; event and, 16,
175; media, 115, 129; of
potential, 80; self and, 125
ethics, 18, 21, 43–6, 100, 124,
143, 152; affect and, 11, 34,
36, 209; care and, 198–200
event, 47–8, 52–3, 58, 60, 119,
128, 145, 169, 182–3,
190–3; aesthetic politics and,
68, 70; affect and, 47, 63,
91–3, 96, 115, 205–6;
biogram and, 117; body and,
49, 54–6, 211; care and,
165–6, 196–8, 202;
difference and, 95; ecology
and, 125, 137, 152, 168,
202; emergence and, 156,
170; experience and, 13,
126, 157; immediation and,
147, 149, 151; micropolitics
and, 79–80; mutual inclusion
and, 187, 214; politics and,
144; potential and, 172;
relation and, ix, 50, 97, 163,
186, 215; thinking-feeling
and, 94; thought and, 194–5;
time and, 136; value and,
153, 201; virtual and, 189
experience, 129, 131, 142, 149,
212; affect and, 1, 4–5, 8,
49, 51, 147–8, 207, 210–11;
belonging and, 45; body and,
14, 44, 55; capitalism and,
23–4; duration and, 61–3;

Index

experience (cont.)

ecology and, 127, 153; event and, 13, 126, 157; field of, 122, 181; human and, 150; incipiency and, 189; intensity and, 6, 38, 42, 73, 76, 140, 181, 204; micropolitics and, 79; potential and, 31; process of, 174; rationality and, 114; subject and, 52; surplus-value and, 101; transindividual and, 163

experimentation, 2–3, 78, 98, 111, 124, 144, 161, 170–1, 174–6; technique and, 135, 169

expression, 130, 132, 154, 161, 172, 174–5, 186, 197–8, 200; affect and, 8, 11, 31–2, 205–8, 212–14; body and, 45; creativity and, 177; ecology and, 149, 202; ideology and, 93; language and, 13, 73, 77, 213; potential and, 176, 201; tendency and, 189; virtual and, 188

fascism, 65–6, 82, 104, 144; affect and, 209; micro-, 101, 103, 106, 108

fear, 35–6, 56, 58; capitalism and, 21, 30; media and, 32

feedback, 210, 213; capitalism and, 29–30; media and, 31–2

feeling, 4, 49–52, 55, 60, 67, 91, 93–4, 125, 163, 208; affect and, 48, 60, 85–6; body and, 9–10; event and, 128; immediation and, 147; life and, vii; microperception and, 53, 58; movement, 141; perception and, 77, 120. *See also* affect; intensity; thinking-feeling

field, 17, 20, 48, 99–100, 115–17, 145, 159; activity and, 105; aesthetic and, 175; affect and, 124, 148; attunement and, 106; belonging and, 18; of capitalism, 41; of conditions, 52; contrast and, 107; emergence and, 103–4, 108; of events, 89; of life, 109, 111, 114, 117; of potential, 19, 170, 194–5, 199; of resistance, 111; of resonance, 123; social, 25, 43; of thresholds, 26. *See also* relational field

force, 60, 77, 86, 113, 138, 144, 148, 158, 194; affect and, 92, 168, 205, 207; capitalism and, 89; event and, 135–6; future and, 155–6; habit and, 64, 66; of invention, 181; life and, 140, 152, 192; politics and, 150; reactive, 103; of speciation, 123; virtual and, 142

Foucault, Michel, 19–20, 92, 104, 116, 144

free radical, 135–7, 141–2

freedom, 1, 5–7, 10, 14, 16–17, 19, 34, 37, 40, 103–5, 107, 111, 158; affect and, 100, 213–15; body and, 97–8; constraint and, x, 12, 39, 72, 195; relation and, 161, 203

future, 1–3, 17, 46, 49, 59–62, 64, 118–19, 182; activity and, 211; body and, 54, 57;

Index

Index

Index

ontopower, x, 64, 69, 116–17; capitalism and, 110–11. *See also* biopower; power
oppression, 10, 35, 85, 101–3, 107; structure and, 104
Oury, Jean, 162

past, 8, 17, 50, 53, 59–61, 118–19, 155–7, 214; body and, 49, 54, 179; event and, 64, 149, 152, 182; immediation and, 147–8; memory and, 59. *See also* future; memory; present; time
perception, 160, 180, 185–6, 208; abduction and, 194–5; affect and, 64; autism and, 127; consciousness and, 60; feeling and, 77, 120; human and, 197–8; intensity and, 73; language and, 12–14; non-sensuous, 149, 187–8, 191, 211; potential and, 58, 67; relational field and, 181; virtual and, 118, 200. *See also* microperception
performance, 34–6, 107
Pierce, Charles Sanders, 9–10, 53, 54–5, 94, 194
philosophy, viii, xi, 77–8, 157; activist, 154
politics, xi, 144–5, 152, 173; activity and, 42; aesthetic, 34, 36, 66–8, 100, 106, 174, 202–3; alter-, 57, 113; care and, 198–200; economy and, 1; embodiment and, 51; event and, 78, 97, 201; identity and, 126–7, 143; in-formation and, 150; language and, 69–70;

potential and, 58, 176; power and, 31; proto-, 148. *See also* affective politics; macropolitics; micropolitics
potential, 3, 27, 39–41, 62, 135, 184, 214; aesthetic and, 67; affect and, 5, 7, 11, 31, 36, 206–8, 211–13; biogram and, 117, 121; body and, 44–5, 53, 57, 68, 95; capitalism and, 21–2, 25, 30, 89, 108; creativity and, 8, 175; environment and, 80; ethics and, 18; event and, 115, 147, 152, 154, 157, 172, 191, 193; field of, 17, 19, 159–60, 170, 194–5, 199; freedom and, 14; habit and, 59; individual and, 161; life and, 6, 42, 70, 101; mentality and, 196; micropolitics and, 82; movement and, 119; politics and, 57–8, 120, 144, 150, 176; process and, 63–4; relation and, 50, 141, 203; relational field and, 137, 163; value and, 200–1. *See also* affect; virtual
power, 158, 193; affect and, 19, 32, 34–6, 39, 48, 63, 86, 112–13; biopower, 108–11; capitalism and, 19–23, 25, 37, 91, 104, 109–10; control and, 16, 19–20, 25–7, 29–31; disciplinary, 20, 26, 28–30; economy and, 28; of existence, 54, 65–6, 105, 107, 203, 208; force and, 60; freedom and, 16; ideology and, 84, 87; movement and, 29; ontopower and, 64, 69,

Index

resonance (cont.)
  and, 55; priming and, 66;
  tendency and, 189
Riefenstahl, Leni, 143–4
Rifkin, Jeremy, 25
Ruyer, Raymond, 141

Sartre, Jean-Paul, 160
security, 26, 31, 38, 116–17.
  See also insecurity
self (the), 123; body and, 48;
  care and, 201–2;
  environment and, 125
semblance, 119, 185
SenseLab, xi, 70, 73, 77, 80,
  98, 121–3, 139, 148, 157,
  159, 164–6, 168–70, 174–5,
  177; 'Generating the
  Impossible', 133–7, 140
shock, 53–5, 60–1, 63, 65, 74,
  128–9. See also
  microperception
Simondon, Gilbert, viii, 123,
  141, 158–60, 162–3, 170–1,
  173, 200–01
singularity, 82, 99, 147, 156,
  158, 191
society, 26, 33, 39–40, 83–7,
  102–3, 113, 138; capitalism
  and, 88–9, 108
society of control, 16, 19–21,
  25–7, 29–31. See also
  capitalism
speciation, 122–3, 125, 127,
  136, 144
speculative pragmatism, 101,
  157, 165, 211
speculative gesture, 207, 208,
  209, 213
Spinoza, Benedictus de, 11, 44,
  140, 208; on affect, ix, 3–4,

6, 48, 51, 91, 93, 97, 150,
  177, 203
Stengers, Isabelle, 18, 68, 70,
  72, 118
Stern, Daniel, 56, 141
structure, 16, 50, 52, 66, 92,
  104–6, 133, 173, 193;
  capitalism and, 108, 110–11;
  economy and, 137; ideology
  and, 34, 58, 83;
  improvisation and, 135, 175;
  power and, 93, 95–8, 101–4;
  process and, 87–91; self-
  structuring, 88, 99; society
  and, 26, 84–7, 89; of
  thought, 184
subject, 170, 182, 214; affect
  and, 4, 48, 150–1, 210–11;
  care and, 198; emotion and,
  209; event and, 157, 196;
  feeling and, 54; freedom and,
  215; group-, 162–4; human,
  149, 152, 155; individual
  and, 160, 214; object and, x,
  14, 52, 94, 190, 199;
  relation and, 161. See also
  intersubjectivity; object
surplus-value, 191–2;
  capitalism and, 20–1, 28–30;
  creativity and, 208; of life,
  99, 101, 107, 109, 201–2.
  See also value
system, 11, 17, 27, 66, 73,
  100, 113–14, 136; capitalism
  and, 80, 108, 111; economy
  and, 21; versus process, 108,
  111

Tarde, Gabriel, 106
technique, 124, 166, 168; affect
  and, 97, 207, 209–10;

Index

biogram and, 117, 121; event and, 134, 157; of domination, 104; experimentation and, 135, 169; improvisation and, 96, 98. *See also* ecology, of practices; procedure; techniques of relation

techniques of relation, 76–8, 97, 107, 139, 169–71, 202–3. *See also* relation; technique

tendency, 50, 59, 103, 182–3, 211; affect and, 96, 101–2, 105, 122, 202, 205; biogram and, 118, 121; body and, 55, 57, 187; capitalism and, 109; capture and, 104; emergence, 200; event and, 120; incipiency and, 60; individual and, 115–16; life and, 117, 184; mutual inclusion and, 190–2; supernormal, 180–3, 202

terminus, 60, 62, 66–7, 70

terrorism, 29–32, 35. *See also* fear

things-in-the-making, viii–ix

thinking-feeling, x–xi, 67–8, 91, 98, 100–1, 106, 111, 120, 147, 149, 207, 210, 213–14; affect and, 94, 96–7; body and, 101, 211; transindividual and, 94–5. *See also* consciousness; feeling; thought

thought, vii–ix, xi, 5, 7, 9–10, 15, 59–60, 66–7, 77–8, 91, 93, 95, 116, 141–2, 145, 153, 155, 166, 178, 189; event and, 168, 194–5;

structure of, 184. *See also* consciousness; thinking-feeling

threshold, 194–5; affect and, 4, 10, 93, 212; control and, 26; economy and, 137–8; event and, 171, 193; experience and, 210; potential and, 3

time, 49, 60–2, 66, 118, 123, 128–9, 131–2, 136. *See also* duration; future; past; present

Tinbergen, Niko, 180–1

transindividual, 120, 161–4, 171–2, 200–1, 203, 215; affect and, 94–5, 98, 128, 205–6, 209–10. *See also* individual; preindividual

transversality, x–xi, 48–9

value, 99, 133, 140, 144, 153, 165, 186, 190; affect and, 209; care and, 196; life-, 138; potential and, 200–1; process and, 79; relation and, 139. *See also* surplus-value

violence, 35–6, 43

virtual, 13, 67, 189–90, 196, 200; affect and, 5; emergence and, 185–7; event and, 68; expression, 188; force and, 142; image and, 118. *See also* potential

vitality, 10, 141; body and, 152; capitalism and, 22–3, 25

vitality affect, 141, 200

Waltz with Bashir (Folman), 142–5

Index

Whitehead, Alfred North, viii, 98–100, 167; on affect, 61; on concern, 196–8; on contrast, 66–7, 99–100; on decision, 174; on eternal object, 62; *Function of Reason, The,* 153; on immediate past, 59–60; on life, 183; on mentality and physicality, 155–6, 178–9, 182–3, 212; on negative prehension, 55; on non-sensuous perception, 149; on perishing, 151–2; on re-enaction, 147, 155